"Steve Addison masterfully ta[...] to help us discover our plac[...] tions at the end of each chapt[...] our own story intersects with God's story so that we might think and act differently."
—DAVE FERGUSON, LEAD VISIONARY, NEWTHING; AUTHOR OF *B.L.E.S.S: 5 EVERYDAY WAYS TO LOVE YOUR NEIGHBOR AND CHANGE THE WORLD*

"Steve Addison is one of my favorite authors. I read everything he writes. Steve is not only a master chronicler of God's movement upon earth but a practitioner. This book is worth your time and will place you firmly within the center of your calling."
—PEYTON JONES, AUTHOR OF *REACHING THE UNREACHED* AND *CHURCH PLANTOLOGY*

"I love Steve's books! I refer back to them over and over again. Understanding our role in God's story is the foundation for our own pursuit of movements. A must-read!"
—CHRIS GALANOS, AUTHOR OF *FROM MEGACHURCH TO MULTIPLICATION: A CHURCH'S JOURNEY TOWARD MOVEMENT*

"Immensely practical—ideal for disciple-making groups."
—RALPH MOORE, HOPE CHAPEL CHURCHES

"Place this collection of Bible studies in front of your disciples, and watch to see who burns for the Lord's glory among the nations."
—NATHAN SHANK, INTERNATIONAL MISSION BOARD (IMB) STRATEGY LEADER FOR SOUTH ASIAN PEOPLES

YOUR
PART *in*
GOD'S
STORY

Also by Steve Addison

Movements That Change the World: Five Keys to Spreading the Gospel (2009)

What Jesus Started: Joining the Movement, Changing the World (2012)

Pioneering Movements: Leadership That Multiplies Disciples and Churches (2015)

The Rise and Fall of Movements: A Roadmap for Leaders (2019)

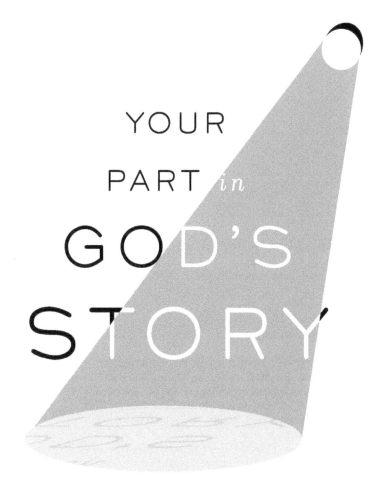

YOUR
PART *in*
GOD'S
STORY

40 DAYS *from* GENESIS *to* REVELATION

STEVE ADDISON

MOVEMENTS
PUBLISHING

First published in 2021 by 100 Movements Publishing
www.100Mpublishing.com
Copyright © 2021 by Steve Addison

www.100Mpublishing.com
www.movementleaderscollective.com
www.catalysechange.org

The author has no responsibility for the persistence or accuracy of URLs for external or third-party internet websites referred to in this book, and does not guarantee that any content on such websites is, or will remain, accurate or appropriate.

All Scripture quotations, unless otherwise indicated, are taken from the New International Version®, NIV®. Copyright ©1973, 1978, 1984, 2011 by Biblica, Inc.™ Used by permission of Zondervan. All rights reserved worldwide. www.zondervan.com. The "NIV" and "New International Version" are trademarks registered in the United States Patent and Trademark Office by Biblica, Inc.™

ISBN: 978-1-7355988-9-5 (paperback)

Cover design: Lindy Martin
Interior design and cover jacket design: Revo Creative Ltd
Editor: Anna Robinson

100 Movements Publishing
An imprint of Movement Leaders Collective
Cody, Wyoming

*Then he opened
their minds
so they could
understand the
Scriptures.*

LUKE 24:45

CONTENTS

WITH JESUS
ON THE ROAD
TO EMMAUS

What could be more important than the mission of God in the world through Jesus Christ?

Yet for over a hundred years, Westerners have been debating what that mission is. We are no clearer today than we were a century ago. It is my conviction that we can only resolve this malaise by returning to the life, ministry, death, and resurrection of Jesus.

"The goal of mission is the glory of God, that he may be known and honored for who he really is."[1] Through the Scriptures, we see the glory of God revealed in the face of Jesus. We see the mission of God lived out and reproduced in his first followers. And we see the risen Lord continuing his mission through the people of God in the power of the Holy Spirit.

This is a book about the mission of God—Father, Son, and Holy Spirit. The story begins in Genesis and ends in Revelation, but its center is found in the life, ministry, death, and resurrection of Jesus. It's his story, yet he invites us to play our part in it.

When Jesus rose from the dead, he encountered a band of defeated, disillusioned, divided followers. Just like us. If Jesus had not risen, Peter, Andrew, James, and John would have returned to their nets, and Matthew to collecting taxes. The disciples would have lived out their lives in obscurity, and we would never have heard of them. There would have been no missionary movement that bears the name of Jesus.

We are no different from those first disciples. Left to our own understanding, our own initiative, and our own resources, the mission of God will flounder. But we aren't left alone: Jesus still leads the way. He takes the worst of sinners and turns them into his representatives.

How does he do that? To find out, let's take a walk with him (Luke 24:13–35).

It was the Sunday after the crucifixion. Two disciples were walking the two-hour journey from Jerusalem to Emmaus. They were discussing all that had happened that day, when a stranger joined them. He appeared to know nothing of the events in Jerusalem, so the disciples told him how Jesus, whom these disciples regarded as a prophet, had been handed over to the Romans and crucified. Their hopes that Jesus would redeem Israel were dashed. Yet only that morning, some of the women had found his tomb empty, and a vision of angels told them Jesus had risen. When the two travelers left Jerusalem that day, the reports had not been confirmed.

The stranger then turned on them, calling them foolish and slow to believe the prophets, who had foretold that the Messiah would suffer before entering his glory. Then, beginning with Moses and all the Prophets, he explained what the Scriptures taught about himself—for this stranger was the risen Lord Jesus, but the disciples were kept from recognizing him.

It was almost evening when they arrived at Emmaus, and the stranger made to keep going, but the disciples insisted he stay with them. At the meal, Jesus took bread, gave thanks, broke it, and began to give it to them, just as he had done at the feeding of the five thousand and for the disciples at the last supper.[2] Their eyes were opened, and they realized it was Jesus, but suddenly he was gone. Though the hour was late, their hearts were on fire, and they immediately headed back to Jerusalem to find the apostles.

Jesus was alive!

Despite spending three years with him, the disciples had never really understood who Jesus was or how he would fulfil his mission. Even worse, his closest disciples had surrendered to temptation and slept while he prayed at Gethsemane. They fled and denied him at the first sign of danger. They watched him die "at a distance."[3] When Jesus taught them that he would suffer and die in Jerusalem according to the Father's plan, their conversation turned to which of them was the greatest.[4] Disciples like these could only play their part in bearing witness to Jesus through a deep transformation.[5] That is exactly what happened.

We must see ourselves in these men who failed him. We must know that the movement of God does not begin or end with us. We are those fearful, unfaithful disciples until God in his mercy transforms us into his witnesses. That's how we play our part in his story.

Jesus had just forty days to restore the community of disciples and prepare them for a worldwide mission. The account in Luke 24 gives us a glimpse of how he did it. Walking with these two disciples, he unpacked the Scriptures—from Moses to Malachi. Their hearts burned within them, and he opened their minds to understand the great movement of God revealed in his Word that centers on Christ. All of Scripture points to him, and all of Scripture is fulfilled in him—his sufferings, his victory, the mission to proclaim the good news and make disciples of all nations.[6]

Jesus wanted his disciples to understand this *before* he sent his Spirit in power and released them to play their part in God's story.

He could have appeared to thousands, but on that day, Jesus chose just two disciples, not even apostles, one whose name we don't even know. They were walking in a fog of doubt and despair, yet he came to them—just as he comes today to unknown, unnamed disciples, opening our minds and setting our hearts on fire.

My prayer is we'll go on that Emmaus journey together, from the beginning to the end of God's great plan. The Messiah suffered, he rose from the dead on the third day, and repentance for the forgiveness of sins is to be proclaimed to all nations, beginning in Jerusalem. This is God's mission in which we participate in the power of the Holy Spirit.[7]

The 40-Day Challenge

This is your opportunity to spend forty days with Jesus while he teaches you about the mission of God and your part in it.

You'll need thirty to forty minutes for each study: ten minutes to read the Scriptures, ten minutes to read the reflection, and ten minutes to respond and pray.

Your starting point will be the same as that of the disciples on the road to Emmaus: his living Word and his presence.

On the journey from Genesis to Revelation, we'll look at forty decisive moments. If you understand those moments, you'll understand God's story and your place in it.

Let the Word and the Spirit do their work in you. Become a different person through your encounters with Jesus on the Emmaus road.

Don't take this journey alone—see if others will go with you. Jesus shapes disciples in groups, so meet with others and share what you're learning. You can even do some or all of the studies together.

This is not a book about practical steps and methods; there are other books for that.[8] This is a book about God and his purposes, and how he shapes us to play our part in them. As the Word and the Spirit do their work, and you obey, the rest will follow.

Trust Jesus to do for you what he did for those early disciples. He found them in their failure; he opened their minds to understand God's mission; he showed them their part in God's story; he promised the power of the Holy Spirit; and he set them loose on the world.

Jesus doesn't choose superheroes. He chooses ordinary people, and then he shapes them to play their part in his story.

This book is an invitation to that journey of discovery.

On page 251, there are instructions on how to complete the 40-Day Challenge for individuals and groups.

Let's begin.

*By the word
of the LORD the
heavens were
made, their starry
host by the breath of
his mouth.*

PSALM 33:6

I

THE BEGINNING

Read GENESIS 1—3

God created the heavens and the earth from nothing. The earth was without form, covered in darkness, and the Spirit of God hovered over the waters. God's first recorded words declare, "Let there be light!"—a bright canvas on which to display his glory. He created effortlessly by his Word, and the earth was brimming with life—the fish of the sea, the animals roaming the land, the birds of the air. Creation is good, but it is not divine. The sun, moon, and the stars are not gods to be worshiped but lights hung in the sky by the one, true God.

The pinnacle of all God's creation was humanity, the goal to which everything was directed.[1] On the sixth day, the Lord formed a man from the dust of the ground, and breathed into him the very breath of God, the breath of life. Man as male and female uniquely display God's image—they are made for relationship with him.

That relationship was a gift, but it was maintained by faithful obedience to God's Word. The man and the woman he made could eat freely from any tree in the garden, but they must not eat from the tree of the knowledge of good and evil or they would die.

Eden was a garden planted by the Lord for the man and the woman to enjoy. The garden was the place where heaven and earth met.[2] In this garden-temple, humanity was both priest and king,[3] walking with God, bringing his rule, and obeying his Word. Adam was to work and take care of the garden—words that later refer to Old Testament priests and their work in the tabernacle and temple. At first, Adam ruled the garden for God, and then he extended God's reign over the whole earth.[4]

God gave humanity a part to play: they were to push out beyond the boundaries of Eden and fill the earth with his glory. The man and the woman must live by faith in God's Word and obey him. Through their obedience, they would reflect his image and glory, and God's nature would be displayed throughout the world.[5] Everything depended on this.

Into this ideal world came the Tempter in the form of one of God's creatures, a snake. He opened a discussion with Eve on the meaning and significance of God's command. The Serpent asked, "Did God really say?" questioning the truthfulness of God's Word. He cast doubt on the character of a God who restricts human freedom and assured Eve if she ate from the tree she would not die. Instead, she would become like God, deciding for herself what is right and wrong.

Sin is the refusal to trust God's goodness and obey his Word. It is the dethroning of God, so we might rule in his place. Through their betrayal, Adam and Eve exchanged God's loving rule for Satan's domination, and the whole created order was subject to futility (Romans 8:20).

Ashamed, the man and woman hid from God, fearing his rejection, refusing to cast themselves on his mercy. Yet a merciful God came looking for them, calling out, "Where are you?" and asking, "What is this you have done?" Adam and Eve didn't ask for forgiveness. Instead, they denied responsibility. The woman blamed the Serpent. The man blamed the "woman *you* put here with me."

Adam and Eve put their word above God's Word, and death came into the world. Relationships were shattered between God and his image bearers, between men and women, between humanity and the earth. "With sin God's curse enters creation alongside God's blessing."[6] Life would now be plagued by shame, hardship, pain, and conflict. Through the man and the woman, Satan gained control of everything placed by God under their authority. Satan usurped God's authority and set himself up as the prince of this world.[7]

As God's priests and kings, Adam and Eve had the authority to drive the Serpent from the garden, but instead *they* were expelled. The ones who should have extended God's dwelling place throughout the earth were excluded from God's presence.[8] They had a part to play, and they failed.

But the story didn't end there.

God continued to shape them as they experienced both his justice and mercy. Judgment was not God's last word. God promised that a descendant or "seed" would come from the woman. The mission to fill the earth with God's glory would continue, but in a different way. God had a plan. He set out on a mission to rescue "sinful, but repentant, people from the power of sin and death."[9] This is the story that unites all the stories of Scripture. The battle against evil is won through suffering. The Serpent will strike his heel, but the offspring of the woman will crush the Serpent's head.

Genesis 3 ends in an act of faith and hope. Adam names the woman *Eve*, for she will become the mother of all the living. She will bear the offspring who is the hope of God's image bearers, the One who dies in their place, the One who will crush the Serpent's head, and fill heaven and earth with the glory of God.

YOUR PART IN GOD'S STORY

1. What are you learning about God and his mission?

_____

_____

_____

_____

_____

_____

2. How does God shape the people he calls?

_____

_____

_____

_____

_____

_____

_____

3. What is God saying to you about your part in his story?

_____

_____

_____

_____

_____

_____

_____

4. How will you think and act differently?

_____

_____

_____

_____

_____

_____

_____

_____

As people moved eastward, they found a plain in Shinar and settled there.

GENESIS 11:2

2

WE'LL MAKE
A NAME FOR
OURSELVES

Read GENESIS 11:1—9

The first man and woman traded loving obedience for the chance to become like God. Relationships with God, others, and the created order were broken, and death reigned. Genesis 1–11 shows a recurring pattern in human history—sin, followed by God's judgment, tempered with mercy, then worsening sin. Despite judgment, despite mercy, the cycle continued.

Sin entered the world and, like a predator, is crouching at the door ready to strike and control (Genesis 4:7). Cain succumbed and murdered his brother. Abel's blood cried out to the Lord from the ground, the land was cursed, and Cain was condemned to a life of wandering. Yet in his mercy, God placed a mark of protection upon Cain.[1]

In the story of creation, we heard again and again that, "God saw that it was good," and, "God saw all that he had made and it was very good" (Genesis 1). But by the time of Noah we read, "The LORD saw how great the wickedness of the human race had become on the earth, and that every inclination of the thoughts of the human heart was only evil all the time" (Genesis 6:5). Instead of the glory of God, violence was everywhere.[2]

As the people migrated further east from Eden, they settled on the plain of Shinar between the Tigris and Euphrates rivers. There they set about building a city and a tower that would reach to the heavens. Eden was meant to be the place where heaven and earth met. God wanted to make the whole earth his dwelling place by filling it with his image bearers.[3] The first man, Adam, received his name from God. But these men sought to make a name for themselves in defiance of God. They settled and resisted being scattered as God intended. They built a city where God had no place. They dug in and stormed heaven. Like Adam and Eve, they sought to be like God.

Humanity's rebellion came to a head at the Tower of Babel. In their Akkadian language, *Babel* (Babylon) means *gate of the gods*. But in Hebrew, *Babel* sounds similar to *balal,* the word for *confusion.*[4] God brought confusion upon their attempts to reach the heavens.

Babel represents our failure when we try to go it alone in defiance of our Creator.[5] In Scripture, Babylon came to represent a godless society that persecuted God's people, and was given to pleasures, wealth, superstitions, and judgment.[6] The tower was a Mesopotamian ziggurat, an artificial mountain with a staircase structure leading up to a temple, which linked heaven and earth. However, it was not the tower but Babylon's sin that reached the heavens.

God was not impressed with this tower. It was so small that he had to come down before he could even see it! Defiance was met with judgment. God confused their speech and scattered them across the face of the earth. He was their Creator, and the Lord over human history. Their project was over.

Humanity is forever returning to the Tower of Babel. Judgment follows when we resist God's plan. He disciplines those he loves and is active in the world to limit the spread of sin in the lives of individuals, groups, and nations. He is the

Father waiting for his prodigal sons and daughters to come to their senses and return home.

As the story of Babel ends, we are left wondering, *what next?* Is this all there is to human history: sin, judgment, and mercy followed by a new cycle of sin and judgment? Though all the other stories of judgment in Genesis 3–11 were tempered by grace, there is no word of grace in the story of Babel. Is judgment God's final word? Is there any hope for his relationship with humanity?

The answer comes in the call of Abraham, father of Israel, a plan only God could have thought of. He sees "an elderly, childless couple in the land of Babel" and chooses them to play a part in his mission to redeem a lost world.[7]

YOUR PART IN GOD'S STORY

1. What are you learning about God and his mission?

_____

_____

_____

_____

_____

_____

_____

2. How does God shape the people he calls?

_____

_____

_____

_____

_____

_____

_____

3. What is God saying to you about your part in his story?

_____

_____

_____

_____

_____

_____

_____

_____

4. How will you think and act differently?

_____

_____

_____

_____

_____

_____

_____

_____

All peoples on earth will be blessed through you.

GENESIS 12:3

3

FATHER OF
A NATION

Read GENESIS 12:1–3; 22:1–19

The calling of Abraham was God's response to the endless cycle of sin and judgment tempered by mercy.[1] God chose Abraham and called out a nation for the same reason he sent his Son— he loves the *whole* world. The story of the Bible does not begin with Israel, God's chosen people. The story begins with humanity, made in God's image. God called Abraham to be the father of a nation because he wanted to bless *all* nations— not just nation states but clans, tribes, and people groups.[2] Through Adam, one man's disobedience brought shame and death upon humanity. Through Abraham, one man's faith and obedience will eventually bring blessing and life to all.

Abraham was "a wandering Aramean," chosen from a family who worshiped other gods.[3] Through Abraham and his descendants, God planned to undo the destruction brought through Adam's sin and establish his rule on the earth.[4]

This new chapter in the story of salvation began in the same way as the story of creation—with God speaking.[5] God took the initiative in calling Abraham. The phrase "*I will* …" is repeated six times in three verses. God is the initiator. But Abraham has to play his part in God's story by responding to his calling with faith and obedience (Hebrews 11:8). Abraham must leave the land of Babylon, his people and his father's household, and journey to the land God will show him. This is a radical break with the human attempt to scale the heavens. The builders of Babel sought to make a name for themselves, but it is God who will make Abraham's name great. To play his part, Abraham must trust that God will fulfil his promises and make Abraham a great nation that will bless all the peoples of the earth.

In response to the unending cycle of sin and judgment, God acted with mercy. He chose a man and a woman, Abraham and Sarah, to raise up a nation that will bring salvation to the world. God has not given up on his image bearers or his intention to fill the earth with his glory.

After a long delay and many trials, God fulfilled his promise of a son through Sarah. Then God tested Abraham's faith and obedience beyond imagination. The promises to Abraham were grounded solely in the initiative of God; now Abraham's faith and obedience must be united with God's purposes. With no explanation, God asks Abraham to take his only son, the son he loves, Isaac, and offer him as a burnt sacrifice.

Early the next morning Abraham took Isaac, two servants, and wood for an offering, and left for the mountain that God would show him. Three days later, they arrived at the mountain. Leaving the donkey with the servants, Abraham told the servants he and Isaac would return once they had worshiped. He laid the wood on his son's back, Abraham carried a fire and the knife, and together they walked up the mountain.

Isaac was confused. They had fire, they had wood, but where was the lamb for the sacrifice? His father told him that God would provide.

They arrived at the place of sacrifice. Abraham built the altar and laid the wood on it. He bound his son and laid him on the altar. By now, Isaac knew what was going to happen. He too submitted to God's command and allowed himself to be bound and placed on the altar.

Abraham raised the knife, offering up his son and all his hopes. Before the knife fell, the angel of the Lord cried out, "Abraham, Abraham! Do not lay your hand on the boy … for now I know that you fear God."

Abraham's heart had been laid bare, his faith tested, his obedience proven.

Looking up, Abraham saw a ram caught in a thicket by his horns. The Lord had provided the sacrifice, and Abraham offered up the ram as a burnt offering. Father and son returned to the servants just as Abraham said they would.

The Lord swore by his own name to fulfil his promises to Abraham: Abraham will be blessed and his descendants will be as many as the stars of heaven and the sand by the seashore. Previously, Abraham's responses to God's call had been inconsistent—sometimes he trusted and obeyed; other times he took matters into his own hands. But on the mountain, Abraham's faith was shown in obedience.

Abraham's willingness to sacrifice pointed forward to God's great gift of his only and dearly loved Son, whose death would become an atoning sacrifice for the sins of the world. Jesus fulfils the promise that, through Abraham's descendants, God will bless all the peoples of the world.[6]

God called Abraham, and then he shaped his heart to prepare him to become the father of a great nation. Abraham learned that true faith is expressed in sacrificial obedience. Abraham was declared righteous, not because he was without sin, but because he was made righteous by faith, a faith that was tested and proved true.[7] This is how Abraham discovered his part in God's story.

YOUR PART IN GOD'S STORY

1. What are you learning about God and his mission?

_____

_____

_____

_____

_____

_____

_____

2. How does God shape the people he calls?

_____

_____

_____

_____

_____

_____

_____

3. What is God saying to you about your part in his story?

_____

_____

_____

_____

_____

_____

_____

4. How will you think and act differently?

_____

_____

_____

_____

_____

_____

_____

When Israel was a child, I loved him, and out of Egypt I called my son.

HOSEA 11:1

4

OUT OF EGYPT

Read EXODUS 2–3; 14

God commanded humanity to multiply and fill the earth (Genesis 1:28). He promised Abraham that his descendants would be as numerous as the stars (Genesis 26:4) and that God would make them into a great nation (Genesis 12:2). In fulfilment of God's plan, Israel entered Egypt as a family and became a nation. Yet Pharaoh set himself against God's purpose by enslaving God's people and murdering their offspring.

Afraid of Israel's growing numbers, Pharaoh had every Hebrew baby boy thrown in the Nile. Moses should have been drowned at birth, but his mother hid him for three months, and then, in desperation, she put him into a papyrus basket coated with tar and sent him floating down the Nile. Pharaoh's daughter found him, pulled him out of the water, and Moses became a prince of Egypt.

What followed were long years of preparation—born into slavery, a prince in Pharaoh's household, then on the run as a failed liberator of his people, and finally a quiet life of exile in Midian.

Moses would have lived out his years in Midian as a shepherd, but he was God's chosen instrument. At the burning bush, God revealed himself to Moses as Yahweh, the Lord, the great I AM; the God of Abraham, Isaac, and Jacob, who fulfils his covenant promises and will redeem Israel from captivity.

The Lord had heard the cries of his people and was ready to act.

Moses was still learning that God calls then shapes ordinary people to fulfil his purposes. Moses explained all the reasons he was not up to the task. Chief among them was his inability to communicate. God responded with a question: "Who gave human beings their mouths, Moses?" (Exodus 4:11).

Yahweh has chosen Israel, and he will liberate them. He has chosen them for a missionary purpose: to make his name known to the world. Through the battle with Pharaoh and Egypt's gods, the Lord will reveal his glory to Israel, to Egypt, and the world. When confronted by Moses' demands, Pharaoh wanted to know, "Who is the LORD, that I should obey him and let Israel go?" (Exodus 5:2).

He was about to find out.

God told Pharaoh through Moses, "I have raised you up for this very purpose, that I might show you my power and that my name might be proclaimed in all the earth" (Exodus 9:16).

The Pharaohs of Egypt declared themselves to be gods. The Lord will humble this Pharaoh just as he humbled the builders of the Tower of Babel. God will judge Egypt for her oppression of his people, and he will redeem Israel. The world will come to know the Lord, and what kind of God he is.[1] He is Lord over Pharaoh. He is Lord over creation and over the chariots, horsemen, and troops of Egypt. The gods of Egypt are powerless to save. Pharaoh will be humbled, Egypt will be judged, and Israel will be saved. The world will know who the Lord is.

Israel was saved by faith. Their part in God's story was to believe what Yahweh had spoken, and believe it enough to slay the Passover lamb and smear its blood on their houses where they ate the Passover (Exodus 12). "The sacrifice of the animal atones for the sin of the people, the blood smeared on the doorposts purifies those within the house, and the sacrificial meat … makes holy all who eat it."[2] Judgment fell on the Passover lamb, and Israel was saved.

Israel was not alone in her deliverance. During the plagues, some Egyptians "feared the word of the LORD" and acted to protect themselves; others didn't and suffered the consequences (Exodus 9:20–21). Some Egyptians may have followed the example of their Israelite neighbors and applied the blood of a lamb over their doorways, so they too were delivered.[3] We know for certain that "many other people" from Egypt joined with Israel in the exodus (Exodus 12:38). The plagues had brought both judgment and mercy to Egypt.

The Lord declared what he would do:

I will bring you out …
I will free you …
I will redeem you …
I will take you as my own people …
I will be your God …
Then you will know that I am the LORD your God, who
    brought you out from under the yoke of the Egyptians.
Exodus 6:6–7

Because of his great love, God chose a nation of slaves to be his people, revealing his glory to the nations that they too might be saved. God promised Abraham he would have descendants that could not be counted, a great nation that would bless the whole world by making him known. Now in the wilderness, Israel must discover what that means.

YOUR PART IN GOD'S STORY

1. What are you learning about God and his mission?

_____

_____

_____

_____

_____

_____

2. How does God shape the people he calls?

_____

_____

_____

_____

_____

_____

_____

3. What is God saying to you about your part in his story?

_____

_____

_____

_____

_____

_____

_____

4. How will you think and act differently?

_____

_____

_____

_____

_____

_____

_____

*You yourselves
have seen what
I did to Egypt, and
how I carried you
on eagles' wings and
brought you to myself.*

EXODUS 19:4

5

A KINGDOM OF PRIESTS

Read EXODUS 19:1—6; 20:1—21

At the exodus, God judged Egypt and rescued Israel. Israel did not have to fight for their liberation; God set them free. In a reminder of his promises to Abraham, God told Israel that if they obeyed him and kept his covenant, then among all the peoples of the earth, they would be his treasured possession; a priestly kingdom, a holy nation. Israel's collective life was to reveal Yahweh's lordship over the whole world.[1]

This statement of Israel's identity comes between the exodus (Exodus 1–18) and the giving of the law through Moses (Exodus 20–24). The Creator and Lord over all the earth has chosen the descendants of Abraham to be his people. Israel stands between God and the nations. As a priestly kingdom, Israel will represent God to the nations, and as a priestly kingdom, Israel will represent the nations to God.

Israel must therefore be holy, reflecting God's character to the world. Chosen by grace, Israel must make God known by obeying his laws and walking in his ways.

Israel had a part to play in God's story—to point beyond itself and be a blessing to all people. There is no direct command to go to the nations, but there is a call to live its life before the nations in such a way that God's name—his character—is revealed. Through Israel, God will reveal his intention to gov-ern all nations.[2] The law was given to show God's people how they should live and how they were to reflect God's character to the world.

The law touches every aspect of life: marriage and sex, treatment of livestock, the conduct of war, care for the poor, family relationships, worship, economic relationships, crim-inal law, ritual purity. Jesus taught that the law could be summed up in two commands—love God with all your heart and love your neighbor as yourself.[3]

The Ten Commandments revealed what it meant to maintain a right relationship with the God who has chosen them. Even the commandments that cover human relation-ships are ultimately about God. Those who steal fail to trust God for their needs. Those who murder usurp God's author-ity over life. Those who commit adultery are not satisfied with the husband or wife God has given them. "Those who violate God's commands proclaim, like Adam, that they are independent and wise enough to determine what should be done."[4]

At the center of Israel's worship was the tabernacle, the place of meeting between Yahweh and his people. God knew his people would not always live up to their calling, and so the tabernacle and the sacrificial system provided purifica-tion from sin. This worked by faith: "Israel must believe that Yahweh really is in the tabernacle, that he really is holy, that sin and uncleanness really do make it dangerous to be near Yahweh, and that the prescribed sacrifice really will atone for sin."[5] Israel must know that the Lord is holy and will judge sin. Obedience leads to blessing and life; disobedience to curse and death.[6] Even when they stray, he will forgive and restore his people to enjoy his presence. Obedience or disobedience, either way, Israel will be a witness to the world. "The Lord seeks to create a people who follow his laws and walk in his ways, and he plants them in the midst of a world that does not know him."[7]

All the nations belong to the Lord, but he has chosen Israel as his special possession.[8] They are saved by his grace and then shaped by his holy love to play their part in his mission.

YOUR PART IN GOD'S STORY

1. What are you learning about God and his mission?

_____

_____

_____

_____

_____

_____

2. How does God shape the people he calls?

_____

_____

_____

_____

_____

_____

_____

3. What is God saying to you about your part in his story?

_____

_____

_____

_____

_____

_____

_____

4. How will you think and act differently?

_____

_____

_____

_____

_____

_____

_____

After removing Saul, he made David their king. God testified concerning him: "I have found David son of Jesse, a man after my own heart; he will do everything I want him to do."

ACTS 13:22

6

YOUR THRONE WILL LAST FOREVER

Read 2 SAMUEL 7:1–17; 11–12:26

The Lord took a shepherd boy, the youngest in his family, and anointed him king over Israel. What followed were years of hard preparation under the kingship of King Saul. David was chosen by God, and yet not recognized. In these hidden years, God was shaping David to play a part in his plan. David served under Saul's flawed leadership, and then lived many years on the run for his life. He refused to grasp the throne by force. Eventually God removed Saul, and David stepped into his calling as king.

Now, in 2 Samuel 7, David is at rest from his enemies. Israel is at peace under his control. David has conquered Jerusalem, made it his capital, and has brought the ark of the covenant to the city. From this city and this king will flow blessing to the entire world.[1]

The Lord had promised to bless the world through Abraham's descendants. Now Yahweh's lordship over the world will be expressed through the rule of King David and his house.[2] This king will help Israel fulfil her calling to be a royal priesthood, a holy nation displaying God's glory to the world.

The word *house* can mean a *building* or it can mean a *dynasty*. David built a palace (house) of cedar for himself, and in gratitude he wanted to build a temple (house) to the Lord. But through the prophet Nathan, the Lord refused the request for a temple—that privilege belonged to the son who will succeed David. Instead, the Lord will establish David's house (dynasty).

Through Nathan, God promises David that he will establish his house and kingdom forever. The Lord will make David's name great. He will be David's father, and David will be his son. When he does wrong, he will be punished, but God's love will never be withdrawn from him.

Hear the echoes of God's promises of blessing to Abraham fulfilled in David: *I will give you a land. I will make your name great. You will have descendants.* God's plan for the salvation of all humanity was advancing.

The covenant with David was one-sided. *I will* is repeated again and again. God initiated and established the relationship. David must maintain the relationship through obedience to the law of Moses. In the same way, God's calling to each one of us is a gift, but we are to respond with faithfulness. If David or his descendants turned from God's ways, God judged them, but unlike Saul, he will never cast them off. The house of David will continue forever.

In his early years, "David reigned over all Israel, doing what was just and right for all his people" (2 Samuel 8:15). If only the story had ended there.

This great king betrayed his people and his God. It began when he chose the comforts of his palace over the hardships of command. At home, while his army was in the field, David spied Bathsheba bathing, lusted for her body, and took her. When she became pregnant, David plotted the death of her husband Uriah—a loyal and noble soldier.

With her husband out of the way, David had Bathsheba brought to him, and she became his wife and bore him a son. Problem solved. But David's actions displeased the Lord.

Faithful to his Word, the Lord sent Nathan to David to pronounce judgment. David had despised God's Word and destroyed Uriah's house by the sword. The Lord's sword would never depart from David's house (2 Samuel 12:9–10).

God calls, but we must not take his love for granted. If we resist him, he will discipline us so that we might turn back to him.

David made no excuses. In deep repentance he cried:

Against you, you only, have I sinned
and done what is evil in your sight;
so you are right in your verdict
and justified when you judge.
Psalm 51:4

God forgave David, but his son to Bathsheba died, and David's house and his nation were torn apart by murder, rape, and civil war.

David was Israel's greatest king, chosen and prepared by God. Yet even he failed in his calling. King David points forward to another King, who will come and perfectly do the will of his Father. He will be a son of Adam, a son of Abraham, and a son of David. Unlike David, he will be an obedient Son. This Servant King will crush the head of the Serpent and usher in a kingdom that will never end. His throne will be established forever.

YOUR PART IN GOD'S STORY

1. What are you learning about God and his mission?

_____

_____

_____

_____

_____

_____

2. How does God shape the people he calls?

_____

_____

_____

_____

_____

_____

_____

3. What is God saying to you about your part in his story?

_____

_____

_____

_____

_____

_____

_____

4. How will you think and act differently?

_____

_____

_____

_____

_____

_____

_____

I will make the nations your inheritance, the ends of the earth your possession.

PSALM 2:8

7

YOU ARE MY SON

Read PSALM 2

God made a covenant with David that he would always have a descendant on the throne (2 Samuel 7). Through the house of David, God established his rule over the earth.[1]

Psalm 2 is a royal psalm that marks the coronation of a Davidic king. At his coronation, the king pledged his loyalty to the covenant and was anointed with oil. God dwelt in Jerusalem, David's city, but his rule extended over all the earth; the world is his footstool.

God reigns, yet Psalm 2 begins with the nations in turmoil. A new king is on the throne, and the nations of the world, their warriors and rulers, are gathered together in rebellion against God and his king.[2] God in heaven laughs at their arrogance and announces he has chosen a king. The Lord says to the descendant of David, "You are my son; today I have become your father." The king's mission is to extend God's rule over all the earth. Despite appearances, God's people can look forward to a time when the promises of this psalm will be fulfilled. The promise to Abraham—that his descendants will be a blessing to the nations—will be realized.

There is a pattern. God chose one person (Abraham), one nation (Israel), one king (David), and one place (Jerusalem).[3] God begins with an individual choice, but his purpose is always universal: the blessing of Abraham will flow to *all* the families of the earth; through Israel, God will make himself known to *all* the nations; and from Jerusalem, his rule will extend to *all* the earth. We understand the part we play by seeing how it fits within God's bigger story.

Jesus was the descendant of Abraham through whom all the nations are blessed. Jesus took on Israel's calling to be a light to the nations. Jesus is the son of David, the Messiah who established God's rule throughout the world.[4]

God rules over the great powers of this world. He is not impressed at their attempts to rebel against his king. The Lord's anointed will smash these rebels like fragile clay pots. He will rule with an iron scepter, the symbol of his authority over the nations. This stark contrast in power between God's anointed king and the nations did not rest on human strength, but in the strength of God.[5]

Psalm 2 casts a vision that was not fulfilled through David's successors. After Judah went into captivity, the line of Davidic kings ended. The hope of worldwide kingship seemed an impossible dream, but God raised up prophets who spoke of a new covenant and promised he would send an "anointed one," the Messiah. As the Son of God and the Messiah, Jesus fulfilled all God's promises to David, as well as the hopes expressed in this psalm.

When Jesus came preaching the kingdom of God, he did so as the King that Israel had been waiting for. At his baptism, the Father declared, "This is my Son!" (Matthew 3:17). Jesus is the Son of God and the Son of David. His baptism was his coronation, and he is the King who extends God's rule over all the nations.

Psalm 2 is one of the most quoted psalms in the New Testament, and it's therefore likely Jesus referred to it when he taught his disciples between the resurrection and ascension (Luke 24). Later in Acts, when the believers faced violent persecution from the ruling authorities, they read Psalm 2 and turned it into prayer (Acts 4:23–31). The believers recalled how the kings and rulers of this earth (Herod and Pilate) conspired against Jesus, just as this psalm predicted. Yet they acknowledged that God was in control. They asked God to extend his kingdom rule over the earth, as they boldly proclaimed the gospel in the power of the Spirit.

Rulers of this world will oppose God's anointed King. They will conspire against him and rise up in rebellion. If we are to play our part in God's story, we need to trust that, despite appearances, God reigns over human history. The Messiah suffered, and his people suffer as they bring the good news to a world in turmoil. But the nations conspire in vain. The Son of David will establish his rule over all the earth.

God begins small, but he always has the whole world on his heart.

YOUR PART IN GOD'S STORY

1. What are you learning about God and his mission?

_____

_____

_____

_____

_____

_____

2. How does God shape the people he calls?

_____

_____

_____

_____

_____

_____

_____

3. What is God saying to you about your part in his story?

_____

_____

_____

_____

_____

_____

_____

4. How will you think and act differently?

_____

_____

_____

_____

_____

_____

_____

In the year that King Uzziah died, I saw the Lord, high and exalted, seated on a throne; and the train of his robe filled the temple.

ISAIAH 6:1

8

I SAW THE LORD

Read ISAIAH 6

The southern kingdom of Judah had not seen a king like Uzziah since the days of King Solomon.[1] Uzziah was a successful military leader who ran the country well. Under his rule, Judah had grown in every way. Like so many other kings, his power and pride were his downfall, and he finished his last years in disgrace.[2]

Now the long reign of this descendant of David is over. It's around 740 BC, and with the great power of Assyria on the rise, Judah is threatened.

In this year, Isaiah sees the Lord, the King, high and exalted. The temple can barely contain the hem of his robe. God is King, and only he is exalted—the fate of the nation doesn't depend on a human king.

In Isaiah's vision, the King is seated on his throne, ready to execute judgment.[3] The angelic seraphim cry, "Holy, holy, holy is the LORD Almighty; the whole earth is full of his glory." With their wings, they cover their eyes lest they look upon the face of God. The doorposts and thresholds shake, and smoke fills the temple.

The glory of God is his holiness revealed. His glory cannot be contained in a temple built with human hands; it covers the whole earth. His people are to be a holy nation that reflects his glory to the world (Exodus 19:6). To worship idols, to indulge in sexual immorality, to oppress the poor is to defile God's name.[4] God in his holiness is pure, upright, and true. When God's glory is revealed, there is judgment for sin.[5] God cannot deny himself; his glory is a revelation of who he is—gracious and merciful, just and holy.

The chasm between a just, holy God and his people is too much for Isaiah to bear. Isaiah chapters 1–5 reveal the nation's sins of injustice, idolatry, greed, drunkenness, and arrogance. Isaiah has pronounced judgment on God's people. Their wickedness is the fruit of forsaking the Lord, and despising the Word of the Holy One of Israel (Isaiah 1:4; 5:24).[6] Now he announces his own doom: "I am ruined! For I am a man of unclean lips, and I live among a people of unclean lips, and my eyes have seen the King, the Lord Almighty." How can he stand before a holy God and live? How can he proclaim God's Word with unclean lips? Somehow sin must be removed if Isaiah and his people are to serve God.[7] They must cast themselves on God's mercy and trust him to change their hearts.

Out of the smoke, a seraph comes flying towards Isaiah with a live coal plucked from the altar. The coal touches Isaiah's lips: his guilt is removed and his sin atoned for. God displays his glory to Isaiah, not to destroy but to save.[8] Surrendered and forgiven, Isaiah is ready to play his part in God's restoration of a holy nation that will reflect his image to the world.

Most messages on Isaiah 6 end here, but there's more.

Isaiah is told to speak to the people, but unlike him, their proud and rebellious hearts stop them from seeking forgiveness. They will not return to the Lord. They will hear but not understand. God will prevent a shallow repentance, and Isaiah's message will prepare Israel for judgment. Cities will lie desolate, houses deserted, fields ruined, and the nation will go into exile. The prophetic warnings will be enacted. The land will vomit them out like the Canaanites before them.[9] If just one tenth of them remain in the land, they will be laid waste again. Then, and only then, will a purified and holy remnant arise.

The Lord tells Isaiah that the nation will be like a forest cut down whose stumps are burned black. Yet a glimmer of hope remains. After judgment, a green shoot will emerge from a blackened stump: a descendant of David will emerge from a judged and devastated Israel.[10]

When the Assyrians came, the regions of the north were the first to be overrun and sent into captivity. With the influx of foreigners to fill the vacuum, Galilee became "Galilee of the nations." Isaiah saw that one day, a light would shine out of Galilee on those walking in darkness (Isaiah 9:1–7).

A descendant of David will come and reign on David's throne, and he will establish his kingdom with justice and righteousness.

YOUR PART IN GOD'S STORY

1. What are you learning about God and his mission?

_____

_____

_____

_____

_____

_____

2. How does God shape the people he calls?

_____

_____

_____

_____

_____

_____

_____

3. What is God saying to you about your part in his story?

_____

_____

_____

_____

_____

_____

_____

_____

4. How will you think and act differently?

_____

_____

_____

_____

_____

_____

_____

_____

*He was
pierced for our
transgressions,
he was crushed
for our iniquities;
the punishment that
brought us peace was on
him, and by his wounds we
are healed.*

ISAIAH 53:5

9

HERE IS MY SERVANT

Read ISAIAH 42:1—9; 52:13—53:12

Israel was the servant of the Lord, chosen to be a light to the nations. But the Lord despaired, "Who is blind but my servant, and deaf like the messenger I send? Who is blind like the one in covenant with me, blind like the servant of the LORD?" (Isaiah 42:19).

Before they entered the promised land, Moses warned Israel they would go into exile if they broke the covenant.[1] But they did not listen. So Israel, the northern kingdom, went into exile, scattered among the nations.

Israel had failed as the servant of the Lord, so the Lord tells Isaiah his plan to send another. This Servant is not the nation but an individual. His mission is to gather Israel back to God and to be a light to the nations so that God's salvation reaches the ends of the earth. This Servant fills God with delight; he is quiet and gentle, faithful and persevering; he does not falter or become discouraged.[2] He not only stands for Israel, he is what Israel should have been.

Through this Servant, the covenants with Abraham, Moses, and David will be fulfilled beyond expectation. The Servant will live out what it means to be in covenant with Yahweh and will complete Israel's mission to reconcile the nations to God (Isaiah 49–55).

How will he fulfil his task? Isaiah prophesies this Servant will be led like a lamb to the slaughter and will take the place of those who have gone astray. Under the law, lambs and other animals were sacrificed in the place of sinners. This same principle is at work in the suffering and death of the Servant. "He will be a new kind of guilt offering that will utterly surpass anything that has gone before."[3] Despised and rejected, the Servant will suffer for those who oppose him. He will be pierced for our transgressions, crushed for our iniquities, and his punishment will bring us peace and healing. The Lord will lay on him all our sins. Those watching will regard him as afflicted by God. Yet it's the Lord's will to crush his righteous Servant; his life is to be a sin offering.[4] On the day of atonement, the high priest sprinkled the ark of the covenant with blood to atone for the sins of the whole community (Leviticus 16:15). But this Servant will make atonement for the whole world.[5]

Once the Servant has laid down his life, God will declare his victory. The Servant will be vindicated and exalted. He will see his offspring. He will return from his mission like a warrior laden with spoil. The one who was despised and rejected will take the place of a conqueror.[6] Through the Servant, a righteous remnant will arise to complete Israel's mission by bringing the news of salvation to the world.[7] God's judgment left a burnt and blackened stump, yet from it a green shoot will emerge.

Jesus' role is unique: he alone is the Servant who suffers for the sins of the world. But he is also the example for those God calls to play their part in his mission. Victory comes only through surrender, suffering, and obedience. Paul saw himself as a servant of the Lord (Romans 1:1), and challenged every believer to follow Jesus' example as a servant who laid down his life (Philippians 2:1–11). God calls then shapes us to fulfil our part in his story. He will teach us humility and obedience, and if we trust him, he will achieve his purposes through us.

YOUR PART IN GOD'S STORY

1. What are you learning about God and his mission?

_____

_____

_____

_____

_____

_____

2. How does God shape the people he calls?

_____

_____

_____

_____

_____

_____

_____

3. What is God saying to you about your part in his story?

_____

_____

_____

_____

_____

_____

_____

4. How will you think and act differently?

_____

_____

_____

_____

_____

_____

_____

Then the LORD
God formed
a man from the
dust of the ground
and breathed into his
nostrils the breath of
life, and the man became
a living being.

GENESIS 2:7

10

THE VALLEY OF
DRY BONES

Read EZEKIEL 37:1—14

The Lord handed the northern kingdom of Israel over to the Assyrians in 722 BC, and Israel went into exile. Then it was Judah's turn. Beginning in 605 BC, Judah was hit with successive waves of destruction at the hands of Babylon. The prophet Ezekiel was among the leading citizens who went into exile. In 586 BC, Jerusalem rebelled for the last time and was crushed. The holy city, the temple, the house of David, and the nation of Judah were destroyed by the might of Babylon. A few survivors were left living among the ruins. God had abandoned his city, his king, his temple, and his nation, and left them to their enemies.

Yahweh had warned them before entering the land: if they broke the covenant, the land would vomit them up, like it had the Canaanites, and he would send them into exile.[1]

Ezekiel lived among a group of exiles by the Kebar River in Babylonia. It was there, in a foreign land, that he recorded his first vision of the holiness, glory, and power of God (Ezekiel 1). For the sake of his glory, the Lord had decreed the fall of Jerusalem, and for the sake of his glory, the Lord will resurrect Judah from the ashes.[2] There is hope because God is present, even in the land of exile.

Sometime later, the powerful hand of God seized Ezekiel once again, and by the Spirit he found himself in a desert valley full of bleached bones glistening in the sun. The scattered bones are the remains of corpses denied a proper burial and left for the birds—an image of death in all its horror and finality.[3]

As Ezekiel looked on, the Lord asked, "Can these bones live?"

Ezekiel answered, "Only you know, Lord." Only God could bring life in such a hopeless situation. God commanded Ezekiel to speak the Word of the Lord to the dry bones. Ezekiel prophesied, and there was a rattling sound as bones reconnected, and flesh and skin formed over them. Bones became bodies, but they were lifeless. Then the Sovereign Lord made his breath or Spirit (*ruach*) enter the bodies, just as he did for Adam at creation (Genesis 2:7). They came to life and stood on their feet as a mighty army of God's people. Yahweh declared to Ezekiel that he will raise Israel from the grave. He will restore his people by his Word and his Spirit. They will know that he has spoken and he has accomplished it.

Israel did nothing to deserve this restoration. God had revealed his glory in judgment, and now he will reveal his glory in mercy. He will once again choose his people and establish his covenant with them. He will forgive their sins, give them new hearts, and breathe his Spirit into them. There will be a new exodus, and he will settle them in the land once more.

These promises were partially fulfilled in the return from exile but awaited the coming of Jesus for completion. He will establish the new covenant in his blood for the forgiveness of sins. God will give his people a new heart and put his Spirit in them, and they will obey him.[4]

When we take God's goodness for granted and forsake his ways, our only hope is to hear his Word again and allow his Spirit to bring life. Our best efforts are not enough; God wants to shape our hearts and disciplines those he loves (Hebrews 12:6). Dry bones come alive in his mercy and grace. Only then can we play our part in his story.

YOUR PART IN GOD'S STORY

1. What are you learning about God and his mission?

_____

_____

_____

_____

_____

_____

2. How does God shape the people he calls?

_____

_____

_____

_____

_____

_____

_____

3. What is God saying to you about your part in his story?

_____

_____

_____

_____

_____

_____

_____

4. How will you think and act differently?

_____

_____

_____

_____

_____

_____

_____

*In my vision at
night I looked,
and there before
me was one like a
son of man, coming
with the clouds of
heaven. He approached
the Ancient of Days and was
led into his presence.*

DANIEL 7:13–14

II

ONE LIKE A
SON OF MAN

Read DANIEL 7:1–14

Before they entered the promised land, the Lord made it clear, if Israel broke the covenant she would be punished. If they did not turn back to him, they would go into exile.

In 605 BC, the Lord handed Jehoiakim, king of Judah over to Nebuchadnezzar, king of Babylon.[1] The armies of Nebuchadnezzar came and surrounded Jerusalem. The city fell, and Nebuchadnezzar took the precious items from the temple and placed them in the temple of his god, Marduk (Daniel 1:1–5).

Daniel was among the first group marched into exile. Conquered by their enemies, their king defeated, the city of David overrun, and the temple plundered, Daniel and the exiles lived outside the promised land as captives of a pagan king.

Fifty years later, Daniel was still in exile, and Belshazzar, son of Nebuchadnezzar, was in power.[2] One night, Daniel's dreams were filled with visions from God. A mighty sea was churned by four winds of heaven. Out of the chaos emerged four great beasts, each more hideous than the last: a lion with the wings of an eagle; a flesh-eating bear; a leopard with four wings and four heads; and finally a ten-horned beast with large iron teeth, which crushed and devoured its victims.

These arrogant beasts represented the great kings and

kingdoms of the world. They ruled with savage violence. If God reigned, how could this be? In the garden of Eden, the man and the woman handed dominion to the Serpent, who now ruled over a humanity plagued by bloodshed and violence. What hope was there for a world given over to so much evil?

Next, Daniel saw the Ancient of Days, seated on his throne, ready to pronounce judgment. His clothing and his hair were a brilliant white. His throne ablaze like fire. Thousands stood before him. The court was seated, and the books were opened.

These arrogant beasts, the kingdoms of this world, were no match for the Creator and Lord of the universe. The Ancient of Days stripped the beasts of their power. One "like a son of man" approached the divine court in the clouds of heaven, and on him was conferred all authority, rule, and dominion. His kingdom will endure forever.[3]

This man is a man as Adam was a man, yet his origin is in heaven. Compared to the beasts he is weak, yet he comes bearing the image of God to restore human dominion over the earth. He shows us how we play our part in God's story. Unlike the beasts, this man does not *grasp* power through violence. In Daniel's vision, God *gives* this man authority over all nations and peoples. His kingdom will never be destroyed. He fulfils what humanity was meant to be and meant to do.

God's holy people are drawn into God's rule and authority. Through the Son of Man all the power and greatness of the kingdoms under heaven will be handed over to the holy people of the Most High. Through this Son of Man, "Humanity will regain the dominion and royal status conferred on it at the beginning."[4] We will complete the task of filling the earth with the glory of God.

The Son of Man was Jesus' favorite way of referring to himself. On one level his listeners thought he was speaking about himself as a son of man, a human being (Psalm 8). Yet Jesus as *the* Son of Man was something more. He had the authority to forgive sins, he was Lord of the Sabbath, he predicted his own suffering and death as a ransom for many, and he predicted his vindication and return in glory.[5]

In the wilderness, Satan offered the Son of Man all the kingdoms of the world, if he would bow down and worship him. Jesus refused, choosing suffering and death instead, and received from the Father all authority in heaven and on earth (Luke 4:1–14). Upon that authority, Jesus commissioned his disciples for a mission to all peoples (Matthew 28:18–20). But he not only commissioned them, he trained them, and sent his Spirit to empower their witness. That mission will be completed at the end of the age, when the Son of Man returns in glory to judge the world.

YOUR PART IN GOD'S STORY

1. What are you learning about God and his mission?

_____

_____

_____

_____

_____

_____

2. How does God shape the people he calls?

_____

_____

_____

_____

_____

_____

_____

3. What is God saying to you about your part in his story?

_____

_____

_____

_____

_____

_____

_____

4. How will you think and act differently?

_____

_____

_____

_____

_____

_____

_____

*The word of
the L<small>ORD</small> came
to Jonah son of
Amittai: "Go to the
great city of Nineveh
and preach against it,
because its wickedness
has come up before me." But
Jonah ran away from the
L<small>ORD</small> and headed for Tarshish.*

JONAH 1:1–2

12

SHOULD I NOT CARE FOR THIS GREAT CITY?

Read JONAH 1—4

Assyrian kings liked to boast in official documents of their cruelty. When their armies overran a city, they delighted in the mutilation and the murder of men, women, and children. The survivors were tied together in long lines and deported to Assyria as slave labor to build their great cities.[1]

So when the Word of the Lord came to Jonah to call the great Assyrian city of Nineveh to repentance, he refused. The risks were too great. If the Ninevites rejected his message, Jonah's death was certain. Or worse for Jonah, if they repented, God might forgive this cruel enemy of Israel.

Nineveh was about six hundred miles to the east as the crow flies. So Jonah sailed as far west as he knew, to Tarshish, over two thousand miles in the wrong direction—the other side of the Mediterranean on the south coast of what is now Spain.

However, God would not give up, so he sent a storm that threatened the ship and the lives of everyone on board. Jonah convinced the crew that he was the cause of their misfortune and they should throw him overboard. Eventually they believed him, tossed him into the water, and the storm ceased.

The pagan sailors feared the Lord, offered up a sacrifice, and made vows to him.

Jonah had his first converts, but who would convert Jonah?

Jonah had a part to play in God's story, but first God needed to reshape his heart. From the belly of a fish, Jonah cried out to the Lord. After three days, the fish vomited him onto dry land, and the Word of the Lord came to Jonah a second time: "Go to Nineveh and proclaim the message I give you." This time, Jonah, the reluctant missionary, obeyed.

For three days, Jonah went throughout Nineveh announcing God's judgment. From king to commoner, the city turned to God: they fasted, put on sackcloth, and sat down in the dust. At the king's urging, the people repented from their evil ways and from their violence, and looked to God for mercy. Nineveh's repentance was met with God's forgiveness.[2] The city was saved.

Jonah's mission was complete, but God was not finished with Jonah.

Bitterness filled Jonah's heart. He knew God would be merciful to these Assyrians, who had shown no mercy to their helpless victims. Jonah wanted to know why God wouldn't punish injustice! Anger consumed him, and he cried, "LORD, take away my life!"

Jonah went outside the city, built a shelter and sat down, hoping that God might still judge Nineveh. The Lord caused a plant to grow up and protect Jonah from the sun. But the next day, God sent a worm that chewed the plant, and it withered. A hot sun rose, and God sent a scorching wind. Jonah's anger returned, and he cried, "I wish I were dead!"

This prophet of God cared for a plant that was here today and gone tomorrow, but he didn't care for a city facing the judgment of God. The story ends with God's question left hanging in the air: "Should I not be concerned for this great city of one hundred and twenty thousand people facing judgment?"

This is the story of the love of God that extends beyond his chosen people to the nations. He loves them, despite their idolatry, violence, and oppression. God was on a mission to save Nineveh from destruction. The pagan sailors were not the obstacle. The storm was not the obstacle. Nineveh's king and people were not the obstacle. The obstacle was God's missionary, Jonah—he lacked God's heart. In the depths of the ocean, Jonah cried out for mercy for himself, but he didn't want God to be merciful to Nineveh. God listened to Jonah's complaint, rescued him, and revealed his own heart. God wants his people to share in his love for the world. They are to bring blessing and salvation to the nations, not keep it to themselves.[3] The God of Israel is the God of the *whole* world.

Wickedness thrives because the Judge of all the earth does not execute judgment immediately. If he did, who could stand? He will judge evil, but he waits. He sends his messengers to offer mercy to those who will turn back to him.[4]

Nineveh's repentance was short-lived. Jonah was "right"— they didn't deserve mercy, but God was gracious. They went back to their old ways. In 612 BC, God sent Babylon to destroy Nineveh for their violence against his people.[5] Yet through Jonah, God gave them a chance, and he gave Jonah a chance to share God's heart for a lost world.

God never gave up on Jonah. First, God called him, and then he went to work on his heart. The story ends with the question unanswered: "Should I not have concern for the great city of Nineveh?"

The Word of the risen Lord still comes to God's people today: "Go to Nineveh. Proclaim the message I give you."

YOUR PART IN GOD'S STORY

1. What are you learning about God and his mission?

_____

_____

_____

_____

_____

_____

2. How does God shape the people he calls?

_____

_____

_____

_____

_____

_____

_____

3. What is God saying to you about your part in his story?

_____

_____

_____

_____

_____

_____

_____

4. How will you think and act differently?

_____

_____

_____

_____

_____

_____

_____

*That which
was from the
beginning, which
we have heard,
which we have seen
with our eyes, which we
have looked at and our
hands have touched—this
we proclaim concerning the
Word of life.*

1 JOHN 1:1

13

IN THE BEGINNING WAS THE WORD

Read JOHN 1:1—18

While the other Gospel writers begin their accounts in history, John begins in eternity. "In the beginning was the Word" echoes the first words of the Hebrew Bible, "In the beginning God." The beginning is the beginning of all things, the beginning of the universe.

In Genesis 1, we repeatedly hear, "and God said ... and it was." In John 1, God creates all things by his Word, and by his Word he makes himself known. This Word *is* God, yet he is *with* God. For all eternity God had the Word abiding with him.[1] "Whatever we can say about God, we can and must say about the Word."[2]

The one God exists as three in perfect unity—Father, Son, and Holy Spirit. From eternity, God is a Father—outgoing and life-giving, delighting in the Son.[3] Jesus says of the Father, "you loved me before the creation of the world" (John 17:24). God is love because eternally God is a community of the Father, Son, and Holy Spirit. God's love for us is the overflow of the love between the Father, Son, and Holy Spirit. The Father loves us as he loves the Son.

In the Psalms we read, "By the word of the LORD the heavens were made, their starry host by the breath [or Spirit] of his mouth" (Psalm 33:6). At creation, the Word went out in the power of the hovering Spirit so that on God's Breath his Word was heard: "Let there be light!"[4] The Word entered history in the person of Jesus of Nazareth.

In the wilderness, God dwelt with Israel in the tabernacle. Now the Word has become flesh and literally pitched his tent among us. God's glory is revealed in the Word made flesh, and that glory was revealed supremely through the cross.[5]

The world depends upon the Word for both its creation and salvation. The light of the Word brings salvation into a world under the power of Satan. Jesus' whole mission was a conflict between light and darkness. The light shone in the darkness of the cross, and the darkness did not overcome it. The light shone on every person and exposed them for who they were. Some hid because their deeds were evil (John 3:19–20); others turned and believed.

The Word became flesh to reveal the glory of God so that all who believe in him would become children of God. Tragically, the Word came into the world he created, but the world did not recognize him. He came home, but his own people did not want to know him. We become God's children in the full sense only when we put our faith in Christ and are born again into his kingdom.[6]

The Word came in grace and truth: grace because God loves a world in rebellion; truth because he is faithful and true to his promises. In giving the law, God revealed himself to Moses as the God of grace and truth, steadfast love and faithfulness (Exodus 34:6). But Moses did not see God's glory, even though he had prayed for it.[7] No one has ever seen God's face, but the Son, who is one with the Father, has made God known.

Jesus is God himself revealing the glory of God to a lost world. We don't live in a nice world that God wants to make nicer. We live in a lost world that God wants to save. The worst thing about sin is that it separates us from God. Jesus is Emmanuel, God with us. His presence brings salvation. His presence is the goal of salvation—that we would know and love him as he really is.[8]

The transformation of this world will not come through human willpower. God took the initiative: the Word became flesh. He came to us on a mission and entered our world, bringing truth and grace, offering to transform those who put their faith in him.[9]

YOUR PART IN GOD'S STORY

1. What are you learning about God and his mission?

_____

_____

_____

_____

_____

_____

2. How does God shape the people he calls?

_____

_____

_____

_____

_____

_____

3. What is God saying to you about your part in his story?

_____

_____

_____

_____

_____

_____

_____

4. How will you think and act differently?

_____

_____

_____

_____

_____

_____

_____

_____

This is my Son,
whom I love;
with him I am
well pleased.

MATTHEW 3:17

14

THE DAY IT BEGAN

Read MATTHEW 3:13—4:11

Jesus left his life in Nazareth, came down out of the Galilean hill country, and joined the crowds heading into the Judean wilderness. The prophets had been silent for four hundred years. Now John the Baptist was in the desert preaching a message of repentance, in light of the coming judgment of God. The people of Israel were going out to him, confessing their sins and submitting to baptism—religious leaders, tax collectors, soldiers, and common people came, no longer safe in their identity as descendants of Abraham.

As the Servant of the Lord, Jesus identified with rebellious Israel under God's judgment.[1] His baptism by John pointed forward to his death as a ransom for many. As he rose from the water, the Spirit descended upon him, and he heard his Father say, "You are my Son, whom I love; with you I am well pleased." These words echo the prophecies of the coming Servant of the Lord and the Messiah in the line of David.[2]

Filled with the Spirit, Jesus left the Jordan and was led into the desert to face hunger, isolation, and Satan. Like Israel, he was tested in the wilderness. Like the man and woman in the garden, he had to answer the Serpent's question: "Did God really say?"

Each temptation struck at Jesus' identity and the nature of his mission. First, Satan goaded Jesus to satisfy his hunger by turning stones into bread. God had tested Israel in the wilderness with hunger, to teach them that obeying him was paramount. A time would come when the crowds, satisfied with the bread Jesus provided, would try to make him king by force (John 6:15). Would Jesus give them the good things of life to gain their loyalty? Jesus walked away from the crowds, who wanted the bread but not the Bread of Life. To this and every temptation, Jesus answered: "It is written!" He would live by every word that came from the mouth of God.

For the second temptation, the devil had Jesus perched high above the temple in Jerusalem. He dared Jesus to throw himself down and force God's rescuing hand. Why not use his miraculous powers to compel belief and win support? Later, as Jesus hung on the cross, passersby mocked him with the same words: "… if you are the Son of God!" (Matthew 27:40). Surely the Messiah could save himself! Jesus had the power to do so, but instead he surrendered to his Father's will. He would not abandon his mission to save his people from their sins (Matthew 1:21).

Finally, Satan took Jesus to a mountaintop and showed him the kingdoms of the world in all their splendor. Jesus could have it all if he would bow down before Satan and worship. Jesus could win the world through political and military power without the cross—if he would bow the knee. Instead, he thundered, "Away from me, Satan! For it is written: 'Worship the Lord your God, and serve him only.'"

Three times Satan tempted Jesus. Three times Jesus answered, "It is written!"

In the crisis of temptation, Jesus placed his life and his mission under the Word of God. Unlike Adam, and unlike Israel, Jesus obeyed God's Word. At his baptism, Jesus was revealed as God's Son, and in the wilderness, he showed what that Sonship meant. This conquering King would fulfil his mission as the Suffering Servant upon whom the Spirit rested

(Isaiah 42). The Holy Spirt led him into the desert to crush the Serpent's head. Victory had been won, and the Spirit led Jesus back into Galilee to launch his mission in power.

The baptism and testing of Jesus mark the boundary between his life in Nazareth and the birth of the new Israel—the new people of God as a missionary movement. Everything was on the line. Everything we need to know about the heart of the movement lies within these two stories. Jesus' baptism and testing reveal his identity as God's much-loved Son—obedient to his Father's Word, dependent on the Holy Spirit, and true to his mission.

Jesus leads the way for us to follow. His baptism and testing show how God calls and then shapes the heart of movement pioneers. Jesus' identity was grounded in his relationship with the Father and the Spirit. As he draws us into that same relationship, he calls us to play our part in his story. He teaches us to follow him to the mountaintop and into the wilderness, and our identity is formed in both places. God will shape us into the likeness of his Son, as we surrender to his Word, depend on his Spirit, and pursue his purposes.

YOUR PART IN GOD'S STORY

1. What are you learning about God and his mission?

_____

_____

_____

_____

_____

_____

2. How does God shape the people he calls?

_____

_____

_____

_____

_____

_____

_____

3. What is God saying to you about your part in his story?

_____

_____

_____

_____

_____

_____

_____

4. How will you think and act differently?

_____

_____

_____

_____

_____

_____

_____

God anointed
Jesus of
Nazareth with
the Holy Spirit and
power, and ... he
went around doing good
and healing all who were
under the power of the devil,
because God was with him.

ACTS 10:38

15

THE SPIRIT OF THE LORD IS UPON ME

Read LUKE 4:14—30

Jesus left the wilderness and returned to Galilee in the power of the Spirit. He came as a warrior, armed with his Father's power, spearheading the attack against the devil and all his works, and calling everyone to decide on whose side of the battle they'll be.[1] Jesus was sent by God as the Spirit-anointed prophet and Messiah, who announced the new era of salvation that he brought.[2]

Going throughout the region, Jesus taught in the synagogues, healed the sick, and cast out demons. He proclaimed the good news of the kingdom, and news about him spread everywhere. As he moved through Galilee, he came to his home town of Nazareth. This was his chance to declare his agenda before friends, neighbors, and relatives.

The synagogue was at the center of religious life. It was the place where the Scriptures were read and taught. Jesus regularly attended synagogues, and he was often asked to teach. On this occasion, the reading was from Isaiah.

Notice the words that recur in Jesus' message. The word *me* is repeated three times: the Spirit of the Lord is upon *me*; he has anointed *me*; he has sent *me*. Jesus is sent to *proclaim*. That word is also mentioned three times. He *proclaims* freedom to the poor—the prisoners, the blind, and the oppressed.

The poor aren't limited to the economically poor.[3] The poor are those who, in their need, cry out to God for deliverance. For Jesus, the poor are those who are regarded as outside the boundaries of God's people—prostitutes, the demonized, tax collectors, and Gentiles. Jesus came to release the prisoners. The Gospels are full of accounts of Jesus releasing those who are captive and oppressed by Satan through illness, demonic control, and sin.[4] The word for *release* elsewhere in the New Testament refers to the release from or forgiveness of sins.[5] This release from sin was at the center of Jesus' mission.

Jesus intentionally stopped short in reading the whole of Isaiah 61:1–2. He left out the last phrase concerning "the day of vengeance of our God," when it was hoped that God would punish Israel's enemies—the Gentile nations. This was to be a day of grace, not judgment.

Jesus was anointed by the Holy Spirit to proclaim this good news and bring the new era of salvation in fulfilment of the Scriptures.[6] The people of Nazareth were pleased by what they heard ... at first. They saw God's favor on Jesus, this son of Joseph, one of their own, yet they didn't fully understand his identity and his mission. Jesus made sure they did.

He reminded his listeners of Elijah and Elisha: Elijah, who was sent to a Gentile widow when there was no shortage of needy widows in Israel; and Elisha, who was sent to Naaman, commander of the armies of Syria, and a leper at a time when there was no shortage of lepers in Israel.[7] These two stories explain what good news to the poor meant for Jesus. He came for the prodigals, those wrongly excluded from the people of God. Jesus came as a doctor for the sick, those who are broken and know their need of God. He came even for those outside Israel.

Now that Nazareth understood what kind of mission Jesus was on, the synagogue erupted with rage. They drove him out of town to throw him off the top of a cliff, the common practice before a stoning. But Jesus walked through the mob and left to continue his mission elsewhere.

He had revealed the true nature of his mission and pointed to how it would end—opposition turning to rage, a violent execution, and a miraculous escape from death.

YOUR PART IN GOD'S STORY

1. What are you learning about God and his mission?

_____

_____

_____

_____

_____

_____

2. How does God shape the people he calls?

_____

_____

_____

_____

_____

_____

3. What is God saying to you about your part in his story?

_____

_____

_____

_____

_____

_____

_____

4. How will you think and act differently?

_____

_____

_____

_____

_____

_____

_____

*Put out into
deep water, and
let down the nets
for a catch.*

LUKE 5:4

16

FISHING FOR PEOPLE

Read LUKE 5:1–11

Jesus announced his mission agenda in the synagogue at Nazareth. Now Luke shows us how the Messiah intends to fulfil it. Jesus calls his first disciples, who will form the nucleus of a missionary movement.

It was morning in the fishing town of Capernaum, and Jesus was teaching by the lake of Galilee. A growing crowd was listening to the Word of God. Nearby, fishermen had pulled their boats up to shore and were untangling and cleaning their nets.

Jesus climbed into Simon Peter's boat and asked him to push off from the shore, so Jesus could teach the pressing crowds from the boat.[1] When he'd finished teaching, Jesus told Peter to push out into the deep and let out his nets for a catch. Peter knew this was pointless—they had been fishing all night and hadn't caught a thing—but he was beginning to respect this carpenter from Nazareth and so replied, "Master ... because you say so, I will."

The result was immediate—nets at breaking point, full of fish. Peter signaled to James and John, his partners in a second boat. Soon, both boats were filled with fish and sinking. Peter's amazement turned to fear. He fell down before Jesus and cried out, "Go away from me, Lord; I am a sinful man!"

Peter's response reminds us of Isaiah, who was in the temple when he saw the Lord and cried out, "Woe to me! I am ruined!" Isaiah cast himself on God's mercy, and his guilt was taken away. Only then was he commissioned to go and preach to his people. Before Peter can fish for people he must face his helplessness, even in the world of fishing, a world in which he normally excels. He too must face his sin and be forgiven. He must learn to obey Jesus' Word and follow him unconditionally.

Jesus came to call sinners to repentance (Luke 19:9–10). He was calling Peter to join him in setting the captives free. Jesus reassured Peter, "Don't be afraid; from now on you will fish for people." The boats were brought to shore. The fish were distributed. Peter, his brother, Andrew, and their partners, James and John, left everything and followed this carpenter from Nazareth, who they've begun to call Master.

In Jesus' day, a disciple chose their rabbi, but Jesus is not a rabbi: he is Lord. He called his disciples with absolute authority, and they dropped everything to follow him. James and John left their father, Zebedee, behind in the boat. Matthew left his tax booth. They left behind wives and children to go on the road with Jesus. Only God can make such demands.

Jesus called them, and then he shaped them to play their part in God's story. They became his constant companions and coworkers. He trained them to do what he did. They learnt to follow him as Lord, deepening their commitment to him. He also trained them to make disciples, not in a classroom, but on the road. There were tests of knowledge, faith, and character. There were breakthroughs and setbacks. There was high praise and scathing rebuke. There was failure and forgiveness. These disciples were made, not born, and it took time in real-life situations.

Around the Twelve was a wider community of disciples, also learning how to play their part in God's story. Jesus said anyone who wants to do the will of his Father was his mother, brother, sister—his family.[2] He called them to serve with him in gathering the lost sheep of Israel. They were the new Israel, the restored people of God. This was the fulfilment of what the prophets foresaw at the end of the age, the renewal of Israel through the coming of the Messiah, the Servant of the Lord, in the power of the Spirit. As Jesus trained these disciples, and sent them out, the missionary movement began to multiply. Jesus envisioned that one day the nations of the world would be drawn into his family as the true descendants of Abraham (Mark 13:10).

Peter was discovering his part in God's story. Overwhelmed in the presence of Jesus, he faced his need for forgiveness, he confronted his inadequacy, and he heard and obeyed Jesus' call to follow him and fish for people. This is the heart of our calling—following Jesus as our King, and letting him teach us to bring others into that same relationship of discipleship. We learn how to love and obey him, and he teaches us to make disciples. That's the core missionary task.

YOUR PART IN GOD'S STORY

1. What are you learning about God and his mission?

_____

_____

_____

_____

_____

_____

2. How does God shape the people he calls?

_____

_____

_____

_____

_____

_____

_____

3. What is God saying to you about your part in his story?

_____

_____

_____

_____

_____

_____

_____

4. How will you think and act differently?

_____

_____

_____

_____

_____

_____

_____

*Whoever has
ears to hear, let
them hear.*

MARK 4:9

17

FOUR SOILS

Read MARK 4:1–20

So far, Mark's account of Jesus' mission has been all action— calling the disciples, driving out spirits, healing the sick, moving from place to place, teaching and preaching, proclaiming the kingdom of God, calling people to repent and believe the good news. The movement was growing.

Word about Jesus was spreading rapidly over the whole region of Galilee. People sought him out from Judea, Jerusalem, Idumea, and the regions across the Jordan and around Tyre and Sidon. As enthusiasm grew, so did the opposition, and the plotting to kill Jesus began.

Jesus was by the lake, where a large crowd had travelled from every town to hear him speak. Sitting in a boat just off the shore, Jesus began teaching them in parables. He starts to teach about the kingdom of God, beginning with the parable of the four soils.

Jesus told this allegory to explain why the gospel of the kingdom is not accepted by everyone and can be met with confusion, lack of understanding, indifference, and even fierce resistance.[1] Jesus' parables are the key to unlocking the message of the kingdom of God. And, because it's the key to understanding all of Jesus' other parables, the parable of the soils is positioned first in Mark's Gospel.

The story is about a farmer who sows a field. In Jesus' day, the method was to sow the seed widely and then plough it in. The farmer sows generously and freely. Some seed falls on the path and is quickly snapped up by birds. Other seed falls on rocky places with little topsoil. It grows quickly, then withers and dies in the hot sun, as its roots are shallow. Other seeds land among thorns. The seeds grow but are later choked by the thorns. There is a progression: the first seed never germinates; the second germinates then dies; the third germinates and grows but doesn't produce any grain.

Other seed falls on good soil: it germinates, it grows, and produces a crop multiplying by thirty, sixty, and a hundredfold.

As a parable about hearing the Word of God, Jesus finished by challenging the crowd to have ears to hear. They must ask themselves which sort of soil they are and act.[2]

Later, when Jesus was alone, the Twelve and others asked him about the parables. They didn't understand them, but they wanted to. Jesus told them that the revelation of God's kingship had been given to them, but those on the outside only heard the stories and didn't grasp their significance. The secret of the kingdom is the secret of the person of Jesus. Only faith can recognize that Jesus of Nazareth is the Son of God.[3] The kingdom of God can only be entered by faith in him.

God is powerfully at work, but many don't see it. They may see the miracles and hear the message of the kingdom, but they don't understand. If they did, they would turn and be forgiven. The parable of the four soils is the key to grasping all parables and therefore understanding Jesus' teaching on the kingdom of God.

Jesus reminded his disciples of Isaiah, who was also called to proclaim God's kingship to a people who did not want to know or obey.[4]

As the farmer came to sow the seed, Jesus has come to proclaim the Word (Mark 1:38). Just as God created by his Word, so Jesus' Word brings the presence and the power of God's kingdom. The coming of the kingdom provokes a crisis of decision. People are divided. Outsiders, such as the Gerasene demoniac or the Gentile centurion, become insiders.[5] Some insiders, such as

Judas, become outsiders. "Hearing, receiving, and bearing fruit are the marks of a disciple of Jesus."[6] These disciples seek Jesus out and want to do the will of his Father. They become Jesus' family (Mark 3:34–35). They discover their part in God's story.

The purpose of teaching in parables is not to hide the truth and prevent people from understanding. The intent is to discover whether hearers will hear and obey Jesus' Word.[7] Faith grows by hearing, understanding, and bearing fruit—or else it withers and decays.[8] How someone responds to Jesus' Word determines whether they will be included or excluded from the kingdom of God.[9]

Satan tried to snatch the Word away from Peter through the threat of persecution, and Peter denied his Lord. Riches and the good life choked the Word that Jesus sowed in the life of the rich young ruler, and he walked away.[10] Jesus came to proclaim the good news in order to make disciples. He loved the crowds, healed them, fed them, and cast out their demons. But he is looking for disciples who hear, obey, and bear fruit. Crowds are fickle, and people will fall away, but God is in control, and there will be a harvest.

Jesus' whole mission was like a parable; its meaning was a mystery even to the disciples.[11] Peter grasped that Jesus was the Messiah, but he couldn't understand the cross. Only after the resurrection did Peter comprehend Jesus' identity and mission.[12] God was gracious and brought him to a deep repentance and a full understanding of who Jesus is. It took time and heartache for Peter to discover his part in God's story. We are no different, and God won't give up on us.

Jesus was rejected by Israel, by the crowds, and by their leadership, and he was deserted by his disciples. Yet God used murderous hostility, inspired by Satan, to achieve his purposes. Through his death and resurrection, Jesus achieved the victory that ushered in a movement that will proclaim his name throughout the world.

YOUR PART IN GOD'S STORY

1. What are you learning about God and his mission?

_____

_____

_____

_____

_____

_____

_____

2. How does God shape the people he calls?

_____

_____

_____

_____

_____

_____

_____

3. What is God saying to you about your part in his story?

_____

_____

_____

_____

_____

_____

_____

4. How will you think and act differently?

_____

_____

_____

_____

_____

_____

_____

_____

I am the good shepherd. The good shepherd lays down his life for the sheep.

JOHN 10:11

18

ON THE ROAD

Read MATTHEW 9:35–10:20

Jesus called his first disciples with the authority of God. He commanded them to follow him and promised to send them out to fish for people (Matthew 4:19).

Jesus was on a mission to the one hundred and seventy-five towns and villages of Galilee. He was moved with gut-wrenching compassion for Galilee's two hundred thousand people. Like Yahweh, Jesus saw Israel as bullied and harassed by leaders who were meant to be their shepherds (Ezekiel 34). So as God had promised, Jesus intervened and rescued them.

Jesus lived his mission before the Twelve, he trained them, and now in this passage in Matthew, he sends them out. Jesus told them that the harvest was plentiful and that they were to pray for the Lord of the harvest to send out workers. Jesus intended that his ministry would become a multiplying movement.

Jesus' ministry was characterized by authority, and before they go, the Twelve receive Jesus' authority for their task. They will do what they have seen him do: drive out demons and heal the sick, even raise the dead. Their message is the same as Jesus' message: repent and believe for the kingdom of heaven has come near.

Matthew doesn't describe what happened on their mission. He focuses our attention on the instructions Jesus gave in two parts to the Twelve: the first part covers the mission to Galilee (Matthew 10:5–16); the second part covers the wider mission after Pentecost to both Jews and Gentiles (Matthew 10:17–22). The account is recorded by Matthew to provide inspiration and instruction for the future mission of the church. The mission of the Twelve can teach us about how we play our part in God's story.

They are not to go north to the Gentile cities of Tyre and Sidon, or east to the Decapolis, or south to the Samaritans. This mission is to the people of the covenant; the mission to the world will come later. The Son of David has come as Israel's King and Redeemer. He has come to gather a faithful remnant before sending them to the nations.[1]

The mission is urgent. They are to travel light with just the basics. They are to trust God to provide food and lodging through those who welcome them and their message.

If the message is not received, they are to shake the dust off their feet as a sign of judgment. When a devout Jew left Gentile territory, he would remove the dust from his feet and clothes, casting off the impurity and avoiding the judgment that was coming upon them. For Jesus' disciples to do this in Jewish towns was to communicate to the inhabitants that they were like pagans under God's judgment.[2] Jesus said it would be worse for the towns that rejected his messengers, than for Sodom and Gomorrah on judgment day.[3] Their eternity depends on their response to Jesus and the messengers he sends.

The disciples shared in Jesus' mission; they will also share in his rejection. The Shepherd is sending his sheep into a wolf pack. The kingdom has come, and it will divide people and provoke opposition. The disciples must be shrewd and beyond reproach.

From verse 17, Jesus moves into instructions that apply to the post-Easter mission to both Jews *and* Gentiles. All his predictions of persecution were fulfilled in the mission of the early church: they'll be flogged in the synagogues, arrested and brought before governors and kings, but the Holy Spirit will give them the words they need in their defense.[4]

We learn from Acts that, after Pentecost, messengers returned to the towns and villages of Judea, Galilee, and Samaria, and planted growing churches in those regions (Acts 9:31). And that was just the beginning!

Jesus called disciples who were willing to follow him and learn how to fish for people. He trained them as he went into towns and villages, healing the sick, casting out demons, proclaiming the kingdom, and calling people to repentance and faith. The disciples weren't perfect, but they were teachable, and Jesus trained their head, heart, and hands. He called them and then shaped them to fulfil God's purposes. They found themselves in God's story by watching Jesus, listening to what he said, and doing what he did.

YOUR PART IN GOD'S STORY

1. What are you learning about God and his mission?

_____

_____

_____

_____

_____

_____

2. How does God shape the people he calls?

_____

_____

_____

_____

_____

_____

3. What is God saying to you about your part in his story?

_____

_____

_____

_____

_____

_____

_____

4. How will you think and act differently?

_____

_____

_____

_____

_____

_____

_____

_____

The King will
reply, "Truly I
tell you, whatever
you did for one of the
least of these brothers
and sisters of mine, you
did for me."

MATTHEW 25:40

19

SHEEP AND GOATS

Read MATTHEW 25:31—46

Jesus' mission to Israel was completed, and it was his final week in Jerusalem. As he walked out of the temple for the last time, he announced its destruction. Jesus headed up towards the Mount of Olives, and his disciples asked him when the temple would be destroyed and what to expect as a sign of the end of the age and of his coming (Matthew 24:1–3).

Seated on the Mount of Olives, overlooking Jerusalem, Jesus answered their question. In his final teaching, he focused on the coming of the glorious Son of Man, and the judgment of the nations at the end of the age.

Jesus identified himself with the heavenly Son of Man who receives the kingdom from the Ancient of Days. This Son of Man, prophesied by Daniel and Zechariah, will come in glory with his angels and judge the nations.[1] He will be seated on his throne as Judge and King. All authority on heaven and earth will be given to him.[2]

He had just told the disciples that, "this gospel of the kingdom will be preached in the whole world as a testimony to all nations, and then the end will come" (Matthew 24:14). Now Jesus explains what will happen when that task is finished, the end has come, and the nations are gathered before the Son of Man for judgment. How will they be judged?

Jesus tells the disciples that eternal life and eternal punishment will depend on how the nations care for the least of his "brothers and sisters."

In ancient Israel, it was typical for sheep and goats to be mixed together during the day. At night they were separated, since sheep can cope with the cold but goats must be herded together for warmth.[3] Middle Eastern sheep were not as white as they are today; some were brown with dark patches, so it took an experienced eye to tell the sheep apart from the goats.[4] Of the two, sheep were prized more highly than goats. They were easier to keep and their wool was more valuable.

In the parable Jesus tells, the sheep are on the right, the place of honor. They receive the blessing of their inheritance from the Father, a kingdom prepared for them since the creation of the world. They have served the King's brothers and sisters—given them food when they were hungry, drink when they were thirsty, clothing when they were naked, companionship when they were sick or in prison. Their service is evidence of their loyalty to the King.

The goats are on the left, the place of dishonor. They are cursed and sent to eternal fire prepared for the devil and his angels. They showed no compassion to the King, revealed in their treatment of the least of his brothers and sisters.

Who are *the least* of the King's brothers and sisters?

The least could refer to anyone who is in need, but nowhere else does Jesus refer to the poor in general as his brothers and sisters. However, he *does* refer to his disciples in those terms. His disciples are his "little ones" (Matthew 10:42; 18:6). Whoever does the will of his Father is his brother and sister and mother (Matthew 12:50). When he sends the Twelve out on mission, he tells them, "Anyone who welcomes you welcomes me," and whoever welcomes Jesus welcomes his Father (Matthew 10:40). His disciples are his brothers (Matthew 28:10). So closely does Jesus identify with his disciples, that on the Damascus road, Saul, who had been threatening the Lord's disciples, heard Jesus say to him, "I am Jesus, whom you are persecuting" (Acts 9:5). How the least of those brothers and sisters are received will reveal a person's relationship to the King. In this passage, "Jesus identifies himself with the fate of his followers and makes compassion for them equivalent to compassion for himself."[5]

Jesus tells his disciples that they will be persecuted and put to death. They will be hated because of him. There will be wars, famines, and earthquakes. Facing persecution, many will fall away from the faith; some will even betray other believers; and some will be deceived by false prophets (Matthew 24:4–13).

In Matthew 25:31–46, Jesus is reassuring his true disciples—his brothers and sisters—that God's enemies will not triumph. The nations will be judged on the basis of how they treat the messengers whom Jesus sends to proclaim the gospel.

Jesus has charged his disciples to make disciples of the nations. After the resurrection, he will do so again (Matthew 28:18–20). As they go, they are to expect hardship and a hostile world, but Jesus promised to be with them the whole way.

YOUR PART IN GOD'S STORY

1. What are you learning about God and his mission?

_____

_____

_____

_____

_____

_____

2. How does God shape the people he calls?

_____

_____

_____

_____

_____

_____

_____

3. What is God saying to you about your part in his story?

_____

_____

_____

_____

_____

_____

_____

4. How will you think and act differently?

_____

_____

_____

_____

_____

_____

_____

Remain in me,
as I also remain
in you. No branch
can bear fruit by
itself; it must remain
in the vine.

JOHN 15:4

20

REMAIN IN ME

Read JOHN 15:1—17

Their final meal was over. Judas had departed into the darkness. Jesus and his disciples were making their way through the narrow streets of Jerusalem to the garden of Gethsemane, where Jesus will pray and wait to be arrested. This is his last opportunity to instruct his disciples. There was so much he could tell them, but he only had time for what was most important, so he began by declaring that he is the true vine.

A great golden vine hung over the entrance of the temple in Jerusalem, reminding worshipers that Israel is the vine God planted, that it might produce good fruit and reveal his glory to the world.[1] It never did, and therefore Israel will be destroyed (Isaiah 5:1–8).[2] Jesus told his disciples that as the true vine, he will produce the fruit the Father seeks.

The Father is the gardener who plants and cares for the vine. Jesus is that vine. His disciples are the branches. As he prepared for his departure, Jesus revealed the secret of fruitfulness, which is to *abide*, or *remain*, in him. Abiding means to be loved by Jesus and to love him in return. As branches, his disciples receive life by being united to the true vine. Bearing fruit is the result of being united to Christ. To be connected to the vine means that the life of Jesus is flowing through his disciples, and this leads to fruitfulness.[3]

Fruitfulness is not a human achievement; it is the outcome of lives that remain in Jesus, keep his commands, and experience his presence through the Spirit.[4] Jesus chose the disciples and appointed them to play their part in God's story. Jesus said the disciples were to *go and bear fruit*—and to *go* most likely refers to making disciples.[5]

Fruitfulness involves both following Christ as Lord and making disciples who learn to follow him (Matthew 4:19). Fruitfulness comes by remaining in him—obeying his Word, and knowing him through the Holy Spirit. Without him we will produce nothing.

His presence is the secret of a multiplying movement that glorifies God. His life in us produces the fruit that endures for eternity—lives transformed into his image for his glory.

Just a short time before Jesus spoke these words, Judas betrayed him. The gardener removes branches that don't remain in the vine, and they will wither and die.

Even branches that are fruitful will be pruned to produce higher-quality fruit. Simon Peter was about to face his most severe pruning. Satan will sift him like wheat (Luke 22:31). Peter will deny his Lord, and Jesus knew it. But Jesus prayed for Peter and knew he would turn back and strengthen his brothers. All the disciples will fail Jesus, but when they return, he will restore them.

Jesus calls us, and he shapes us. Even when we fail him, he will restore us if we turn back.

Five times, Jesus told the disciples to remain in the vine by obeying his commands.

Let my words remain in you.
Keep my commands.
Obey my command to love one another.
Do what I command.
This is my command: love each other.

Disciples of Jesus must love one another as he has loved them (John 13:34). How? By remaining in the love of the Father, and of the Son, and the Holy Spirit. In the Old Testament, only Abraham and Moses were called friends of God; now Jesus calls every disciple his friend.[6]

Jesus was preparing his disciples for his departure and the coming of the Spirit. He was getting them ready for their life together on mission. They must remain in him through loving obedience. They must love one another as he has loved them. They must remain faithful to him and to the missionary task in a hostile world. Remain in him, and the fruit will follow.

At the heart of God's mission is his presence, made possible through Jesus and the Spirit he will send. Throughout the world, God is gathering his people. His presence is both the key to achieving the mission and the goal of the mission. God is Father, Son, and Holy Spirit, and he wants a people who love him and who love one another. Love energizes God's mission, and it is the goal of God's mission—a people for his glory from every tribe, tongue, and nation.

YOUR PART IN GOD'S STORY

1. What are you learning about God and his mission?

_____

_____

_____

_____

_____

_____

_____

2. How does God shape the people he calls?

_____

_____

_____

_____

_____

_____

_____

3. What is God saying to you about your part in his story?

_____

_____

_____

_____

_____

_____

_____

4. How will you think and act differently?

_____

_____

_____

_____

_____

_____

_____

_____

*In this world
you will have
trouble. But
take heart! I have
overcome the world.*

JOHN 16:33

21

EXPECT TROUBLE

Read JOHN 15:18−16:4; 17:11−19

Until now, Jesus has been the lightning rod for opposition. The disciples have not felt the brunt of the attack, but they will soon. Jesus wants to prepare them for the world's hostility. The *world* here is the world in rebellion against God; the world that refuses to believe in Jesus and hates the light he brings.

In the face of this rejection, Jesus prayed that his disciples would remain united with one another, just as he and the Father are united in love and purpose. They are called to love the world and seek its salvation. Yet when disciples are rejected, they may be tempted to withdraw from their mission and turn on one another.

Rejection by the world comes because Jesus has chosen them and they do not belong to the world; they are united with Jesus, and they bear witness to him. The world has rejected Jesus because he exposed their deeds (John 3:20). Even though the towns and cities of Galilee saw the miracles and heard the message, they still would not repent (Matthew 11:20–24).

The world's hatred will not thwart God's plan but fulfils what was written: "They hated me without reason" (Psalm 69:4). So Jesus warns his disciples their mission will be carried out in the face of fierce opposition. They should not fear death, but unfaithfulness.[1]

The disciples are not alone in this hostile environment.

The Holy Spirit will testify about Jesus through his disciples, remind them of Jesus' teaching, and will lead them into the truth of his words (John 16:13).

Jesus prayed for his disciples, who would face persecution.[2] His prayer makes it clear that it is the Father and the Son who will keep the disciples from falling away. The Father will protect them from the evil one by the power of his name. The Father will sanctify them by his Word of truth. To be sanctified is to be shaped by God for his purposes. Jesus perfectly demonstrated this by setting himself apart to do the Father's will and fulfil his mission. As the Father sent Jesus into the world, so Jesus sends his disciples into the world. They are not to withdraw from the world, nor are they to surrender to it, but they are to faithfully play their part in God's story.

Jesus doesn't focus on what the disciples must do to survive persecution; instead, he shines a light on what the Father, Son, and Holy Spirit will do to keep the disciples faithful in their mission. The basis of their peace is the victory of Jesus over the world, which gives comfort in the midst of persecution (John 16:33). Jesus' darkest hour was at the same time his greatest victory. He shares that victory with his disciples in their moment of trial.

After his death, Jesus' disciples huddled together in fear behind locked doors. Like most of us, the disciples lacked the natural courage to endure the threat of rejection, ridicule, and violence. The answer was not more willpower, but their recognition of failure, their restoration by the risen Lord, and the coming of the Holy Spirit, who transformed these fearful disciples into bold witnesses. The solution did not lie within themselves but with the presence of God through the Holy Spirit shaping them into the image of Jesus. That was the secret of their success.

YOUR PART IN GOD'S STORY

1. What are you learning about God and his mission?

_____

_____

_____

_____

_____

_____

2. How does God shape the people he calls?

_____

_____

_____

_____

_____

_____

_____

3. What is God saying to you about your part in his story?

_____

_____

_____

_____

_____

_____

_____

_____

4. How will you think and act differently?

_____

_____

_____

_____

_____

_____

_____

_____

Jesus stood and said in a loud voice, "Let anyone who is thirsty come to me and drink. Whoever believes in me, as Scripture has said, rivers of living water will flow from within them."

JOHN 7:37—38

22

DRENCHED

Read JOHN 15:26−27; 16:5−15

Earlier in his ministry, Jesus visited Jerusalem for the Feast of Tabernacles.[1] It was an annual event to remember Israel's journey through the wilderness and to give thanks at the end of another harvest. The holy city was packed with pilgrims camping out under shelters made of branches.

On each of the seven days of the Feast, a priest drew water from the pool of Siloam in a golden flagon and brought it, in a procession led by the High Priest, to the temple.[2] As they went, trumpets blasted out and choirs sang psalms, accompanied by shouts of "Give thanks to the Lord!" At the morning sacrifice, the water was poured out before the Lord. Israel was giving thanks for the gift of water in the wilderness, for the water given for harvest, and was looking forward to the pouring out of the Holy Spirit in the last days.

It was the last and greatest day of the festival when Jesus stood up in the packed temple courts and cried out, "Let anyone who is thirsty come to me and drink. Whoever believes in me, as Scripture has said, rivers of living water will flow from within them" (John 7:37–38). This was an audacious claim. As the water of life was poured out before God, Jesus claimed *he* is the source of living water. He promised to pour out the Holy Spirit upon anyone who came to him.

Jesus returned to Jerusalem for the final time to face the hour of his glorification through the cross. His disciples were distressed and confused, unable to grasp what his departure meant, and so Jesus reminded them of his earlier promise of the Holy Spirit, another *Paraclete*. It's not easy to find an equivalent to *Paraclete* in English. The term literally means *one called alongside to help*. The closest we can get is someone who acts as an advocate for the defense in court—not a trained lawyer, but a friend or protector. The *Paraclete* is an advocate, a witness, a guide, an encourager, a teacher, who helps through a time of trouble.

Jesus is going to the Father, but he promised to send another Advocate who will be with them as they bear witness to him in a hostile world. He won't leave them as orphans left alone to defend themselves. He will come to them through the Holy Spirit—the life of Christ in them bringing rivers of living water.

The world can't receive the *Paraclete* because the world has rejected Jesus. The gift of the Spirit is made by the Father to those who love and obey his Son—those who believe in him and are committed to following him.[3]

The *Paraclete* is a Teacher who will remind the disciples of what Jesus taught—not only the content of his teaching and the events of his life, but their significance (John 14:26). Through the Spirit, the disciples will understand the meaning of his death and resurrection. He'll not only be beside them, but *in* them. They will experience the risen Christ through his Spirit (John 14:17–18). They will share in his character, power, authority, and mission.

Jesus is not only a past figure in history. He rose from the dead, sent the Spirit, and God's mission continues. The *Paraclete* will bear witness to Jesus through his disciples (John 15:26). As his disciples bear witness to the world, the Spirit will convict the world of sin, righteousness, and judgment. It is the Spirit who calls the world to repentance.

Jesus told his disciples it was *good* that he was going away! He was leaving for their benefit, for he will send the Spirit. Before the Spirit came, "everyone deserted him and fled" (Mark 14:50). After the Spirit came, "they were all filled with the Holy Spirit and spoke the word of God boldly" (Acts 4:31). Jesus' departure was not the end; it was the beginning.

Notice how God the Father sends the Son, and now the Son sends the Spirit. This is God's mission, not ours. Yet Jesus invites us into God's story and sends the Spirit into our lives to equip and strengthen us for the part we play. The Spirit in us changes us from the inside out and empowers us to do God's will in a hostile world. Through the Spirit, Jesus calls us and shapes us to play our part in God's story.

YOUR PART IN GOD'S STORY

1. What are you learning about God and his mission?

_____

_____

_____

_____

_____

_____

2. How does God shape the people he calls?

_____

_____

_____

_____

_____

_____

_____

3. What is God saying to you about your part in his story?

_____

_____

_____

_____

_____

_____

_____

4. How will you think and act differently?

_____

_____

_____

_____

_____

_____

_____

*Now my soul
is troubled, and
what shall I say?
"Father, save me
from this hour"? No, it
was for this very reason I
came to this hour.*

JOHN 12:27

23

SURRENDER

Read MARK 14:32—42

The Passover meal was finished, and it was getting late. Jesus had taken Peter and the two sons of Zebedee and walked out of Jerusalem across the Kidron Valley, then up the slopes of the Mount of Olives to a garden called Gethsemane. The name means *olive press*. It was probably an olive grove surrounded by a stone wall.

Jesus went there regularly, and Judas knew it.[1] Prayer was at the heart of how Jesus fulfilled his calling, and Jesus went to Gethsemane to pray, urging his disciples to also pray as he faced his destiny.

Gethsemane stood between Jesus' prophecy of his disciples' desertion and its fulfilment.[2] He knew what was coming. In anguish and distress, overwhelmed with sadness to the point of death, he asked his disciples to stay and watch with him while he prayed. He didn't want to be alone, and they witnessed some of his agony before falling asleep.

Jesus moved away a short distance and fell face down on the ground. This was the turning point: the Son of God has entered the suffering that will lead to his death.[3] Will the Father intervene and rescue the Son, just as he saved Abraham's beloved son Isaac from death? Jesus asked, "My Father, if it is possible, may this cup be taken from me" (Matthew 26:39).

In the Old Testament, the cup was used to sprinkle the blood of sacrificial victims and to renew the covenant between

God and his people.[4] At the Last Supper, Jesus spoke of his blood as the cup of the new covenant.[5] The cup symbolized his life poured out as an atonement for sin, a ransom that would free the new Israel.

There's also another dimension. Isaiah spoke of the cup of God's judgment:

> *Awake, awake!*
> *Rise up, Jerusalem,*
> *you who have drunk from the hand of the LORD*
> *the cup of his wrath,*
> *you who have drained to its dregs*
> *the goblet that makes people stagger.*
> Isaiah 51:17

Jesus' death is not the death of a tragic martyr. It is his surrender to his Father's will. "Jesus saw himself confronted, not by a cruel destiny but by the judgment of God."[6] The Son of Man came to give his life as a ransom for many (Mark 10:45). The new covenant for the forgiveness of sins will be sealed by his death.

He is the Suffering Servant of Isaiah.

> *He was pierced for our transgressions,*
> *he was crushed for our iniquities;*
> *the punishment that brought us peace was on him,*
> *and by his wounds we are healed.*
> Isaiah 53:5

Anticipating this moment, Jesus had already prayed, "Now my soul is troubled, and what shall I say? 'Father, save me from this hour'? No, it was for this very reason I came to this hour" (John 12:27). Crucifixion was death by horrific torture, but Jesus wasn't recoiling from a violent death. There is something more here. Jesus knew that his arrest, trial, and execution were the will of his Father. Judas, the Jewish leaders, the Roman authorities, and the crowd will play their part, but it is God who determines the outcome.[7]

The Serpent has already entered into Judas Iscariot. Satan has demanded to sift Simon Peter and the other disciples like wheat (Luke 22:31). This is the hour when darkness reigns. Jesus doesn't pray for the strength to endure, but for God to remove the cup. All things are possible for God, but the Father will not remove this cup. Jesus wrestles in prayer to know his Father's will.

His prayer is met with dreadful silence.[8]

While his disciples slept, Jesus prayed, "Not my will but yours." He took the cup, placed it to his lips, and drained its bitter contents. He will do it. He will not run, he will not resist, and at his trial he will offer no defense.

Unlike Adam in the garden, unlike Israel in the wilderness, Jesus is the true Son who will obey his Father. He will fulfil his mission. This is the Son of Man, the Son of God, anointed King, Messiah, taking the form of a Servant, humbling himself and becoming obedient to death—even death on a cross (Philippians 2:6–8). This is the glory of God in Christ.

The first man and woman defied God, but Jesus surrendered and obeyed. The man and woman did not die that day, but the world was subject to death and decay. Jesus reversed the effects of death and decay, and brought forgiveness and life.

Jesus returned one final time to his drowsy disciples and declared, "The hour has come."

The disciples missed their opportunity to follow Jesus' example and lay down their lives for the sake of his name, but it was not the end of the road. When Jesus rose from the dead, he forgave their failure and promised his presence and power through the Holy Spirit as they pursued their part in God's plan. Eventually, many did face jail and death rather than deny him. They discovered that the secret was not human courage but the life of Christ in them, the hope of glory.

YOUR PART IN GOD'S STORY

1. What are you learning about God and his mission?

_____

_____

_____

_____

_____

_____

2. How does God shape the people he calls?

_____

_____

_____

_____

_____

_____

_____

3. What is God saying to you about your part in his story?

_____

_____

_____

_____

_____

_____

_____

4. How will you think and act differently?

_____

_____

_____

_____

_____

_____

_____

*He was led like
a lamb to the
slaughter, and as
a sheep before its
shearers is silent, so he
did not open his mouth.*

ISAIAH 53:7

24

MY GOD, MY GOD!

Read MARK 15:15—41

Wanting to satisfy the crowd, Pilate had Jesus flogged and *handed him over* to be crucified. Jesus had prophesied this would happen: the Son of Man would be *handed over* into human hands to be killed (Mark 9:31). Isaiah also prophesied that the Suffering Servant would be *handed over* for the sake of our sins (Isaiah 53). In the Old Testament, God handed his people over to the Gentiles as judgment for their sin. "God is ultimately behind this handing over."[1] This is God's plan, that Jesus will die, not for *his* sins, but for ours.

Like the Servant in Isaiah, Jesus submitted to his Father's will and went in silence. He hung on the cross, deserted by people, deserted by God—alone. At noon, darkness covered the land for three hours—a sign of God's wrath.[2] Out of the darkness, Jesus cried out, "My God, my God, why have you forsaken me?"

Words can't describe what was happening here, but we must try. Yes, Jesus identified with suffering humanity. He entered into our world and experienced the worst this world can do—the depths of human tragedy. But there is more. Forsaken, he cried out to God, "Why have you forsaken me?" Not "*I feel* forsaken," but "Why *have you* forsaken me?" Jesus was under the judgment of God. His cry was the fulfilment of his Servant mission.

Was the Son separated from the Father? No. "Father, Son and Spirit, are united together and cannot be divided … or set one against another."[3] This is a deep mystery. There is no rift in God, yet Jesus died under the curse of God.[4] The Father did not rescue him. In Christ, God took upon himself the guilt and shame of our sin. In Christ, God—Father, Son, and Holy Spirit—condemned our sin. God turned his face away and poured out his wrath. It was the Lord's will to crush him; his life was an offering for sin (Isaiah 53:10).

Jesus' cry of abandonment came from the depths of God's heart. "The Father, Son and Holy Spirit were in this cry."[5] Jesus cried out as one of us, broken and alienated from God's holy love. He stood in our place and experienced the might of God's opposition to evil. He bore our sin. He won our freedom. His love is beyond comprehension.[6]

It is finished.

With a loud cry, Jesus breathed his last, and the temple curtain was torn in two from top to bottom. The purpose of the temple has been fulfilled and surpassed by Jesus. Now there is free access to God through the work of his Son on the cross.

The pagan centurion who crucified Jesus stepped forward. Looking up at the tortured body of a Galilean carpenter on a Roman cross, he declared, "Surely this man was the Son of God!"

This man under God's judgment is God's Son, revealing God's plan of salvation to the world. This is the good news that must go to the nations. This is God's glory revealed. This is God's story, and we are called to play our part in making it known—everywhere.

YOUR PART IN GOD'S STORY

1. What are you learning about God and his mission?

_____

_____

_____

_____

_____

_____

_____

2. How does God shape the people he calls?

_____

_____

_____

_____

_____

_____

_____

3. What is God saying to you about your part in his story?

_____

_____

_____

_____

_____

_____

_____

4. How will you think and act differently?

_____

_____

_____

_____

_____

_____

_____

After his suffering, he presented himself to them and gave many convincing proofs that he was alive. He appeared to them over a period of forty days and spoke about the kingdom of God.

ACTS 1:3

25

HE OPENED
THEIR MINDS

Read LUKE 24:33—49

It was the Sunday evening following the crucifixion. The disciples were meeting behind locked doors. Early that morning, some of the women had discovered the empty tomb, and Jesus had appeared to them and to Simon. As the disciples tried to make sense of these reports, Cleopas and another disciple arrived with news. It was true: Jesus is risen! They had met him on the road to Emmaus.

Suddenly Jesus stood among them and announced, "Peace be with you." The normal Jewish greeting was filled with the promise of forgiveness for their desertion and denial. Jesus had come to restore the band of disciples, to show them his resurrection was real, to help them understand that the Messiah had to suffer and rise again, and to prepare them to take the good news to the world.

The disciples were afraid and could not believe what was happening. Jesus assured them he wasn't a ghost. He showed them the wounds in his hands and feet. They touched him. He took a piece of broiled fish and ate. His body was real. The foundation of their faith will rest on that reality. Without the resurrection, Jesus died a martyr, not a Savior. Now they saw his death in the light of his resurrection.

He opened their minds to understand the Scriptures—the

Law of Moses, the Prophets, and the Psalms—every major division of the Hebrew Bible. The whole story of God's mission was building to the coming of Jesus, his death and resurrection, and the proclamation of the gospel to the nations.[1] Once the disciples grasped these things, they were ready to begin their mission.[2]

Their message of repentance for the forgiveness of sins was not new. It was John's message, and it was Jesus' message.[3] John the Baptist, Jesus, and the disciples all share in the one mission of God, which is now expanding to include the whole world.[4] The mission Jesus gives his disciples will show us "what the kingdom of God looks like now that Christ has come, died, risen and ascended to the right hand of the Father."[5]

This is the fulfilment of God's plan to deal with sin. The descendant of the woman has crushed the Serpent's head. From Jerusalem, the Word of the Lord will go out to all nations, fulfilling the promise to Abraham that through him all nations would be blessed; and fulfilling the prophecy that the Servant of the Lord will be a light for the Gentiles and, through him, salvation will reach the ends of the earth.[6]

There's just one more thing ...

The same Holy Spirit who came upon Jesus at his baptism will now fill his disciples with power to be his witnesses. Jesus doesn't mention the Spirit by name. The Spirit is the power from on high. He is what the Father has promised. Mystery and anticipation surround this power and this promise. The disciples know that he is coming, and when he comes, he will be full of surprises.

In just forty days, Jesus transformed a defeated group of disciples into fearless witnesses and disciple-makers. Notice how he shaped them over the course of three years, knowing they would fail him. Through failure, they discovered the grace of God. Jesus restored them, he taught them, he gave them their part in God's story, and he promised them the life and power of the Holy Spirit. This is how Jesus launched a missionary movement that will go to the ends of the earth. It's his mission, and he shapes us so that we can play our part in God's story.

YOUR PART IN GOD'S STORY

1. What are you learning about God and his mission?

_____

_____

_____

_____

_____

_____

2. How does God shape the people he calls?

_____

_____

_____

_____

_____

_____

_____

3. What is God saying to you about your part in his story?

_____

_____

_____

_____

_____

_____

_____

4. How will you think and act differently?

_____

_____

_____

_____

_____

_____

_____

*As the Father
has sent me, I
am sending you.*

JOHN 20:21

26

MAKE DISCIPLES
OF ALL NATIONS

Read MATTHEW 28:16—20

The risen Lord brought his disciples back to where it all began in Galilee. They had failed him, but he had forgiven them. They had scattered, but he had restored them. They were disqualified, but he had chosen them.

Satan offered Jesus all the kingdoms of this world. Jesus chose suffering and obedience and won back what humanity had lost. He is the Son of Man, who has been given all authority in heaven and on earth to establish God's kingdom rule (Daniel 7:13–14). The promises to Abraham are fulfilled in Jesus the Messiah and in the mission his disciples will complete before Jesus returns to judge the world.

How will their mission be accomplished? Matthew records just a few lines of explanation, and at its heart are these words: *make disciples of all nations.*

The *nations* are clans, tribes, and people groups with their own culture and identity. They are people without the knowledge of the true and living God.[1] The disciples are to do for the nations what Jesus has done for them. The whole Gospel of Matthew has been building to this point. The disciples are to go. It's not possible to make disciples of the nations without going to them. *Make disciples of **all** nations* assumes a change in location—at least for some. They are to go and not stop going until the job is done.

They are to baptize new disciples into a relationship with God as Father, Son, and Holy Spirit. Baptism is the required response to the proclamation of the gospel. There is one conversion experience, which includes repentance, faith, forgiveness of sins, the gift of the Holy Spirit, and baptism (Acts 2:38). Baptism doesn't save, but in the New Testament there is no such thing as a disciple who is not baptized and learning to obey Christ in community.[2]

They are to teach these new disciples to obey everything Jesus commanded; discipleship means learning to obey Jesus. These are some of Jesus' commands: repent and believe; follow me; be baptized; forgive; love your enemies; honor marriage; make disciples; pray in faith; fear God; give generously. These do not comprise a new law; they flow out of genuine repentance and faith in Christ.

This is the core missionary task: making disciples by going, baptizing, and teaching them to obey what he has commanded. Making new disciples is at the heart of what it means to be a disciple. Failure to make this our priority is a failure of discipleship.

Jesus has commissioned; now he promises: "Surely I am with you always, to the very end of the age." With those few words, Jesus revealed the secret of success in this mission: he will be with them always, in every place, and to the end of time.[3] The Father gave Jesus all authority, and the Son promised his presence through the Holy Spirit. That is all they will need.

From this first band of disciples came a missionary movement that has not ceased since it began two thousand years ago. It will not stop until it reaches every people, tribe, and language.

The Great Commission is simple, clear, and concrete. It marks the completion of Jesus' mission on earth and its continuation by his disciples in the power of the Spirit. They become a remnant in Israel who will go to the nations and draw them into the new people of God. This is the church's primary task between Christ's first coming and his return.[4] Each of us has a part to play in its fulfillment. This is what Jesus did. This is what he trained the disciples to do. This is what the Risen Lord continues to do through his people until he returns.

YOUR PART IN GOD'S STORY

1. What are you learning about God and his mission?

_____

_____

_____

_____

_____

2. How does God shape the people he calls?

_____

_____

_____

_____

_____

_____

_____

3. What is God saying to you about your part in his story?

_____

_____

_____

_____

_____

_____

_____

4. How will you think and act differently?

_____

_____

_____

_____

_____

_____

_____

You will receive power when the Holy Spirit comes on you; and you will be my witnesses in Jerusalem, and in all Judea and Samaria, and to the ends of the earth.

ACTS 1:8

27

YOU WILL RECEIVE POWER

Read ACTS 1:1–11; 2:1–41

The year was AD 30.[1] It was early in the morning, fifty days since Passover, and Pentecost had come, one of the great festivals when Jews gave thanks for the harvest. The city was alive with pilgrims from around Israel and around the world. In the upper room of a large house, one hundred and twenty people were gathered praying, when there was a sound like the blowing of a violent wind from heaven—the Spirit had come. Tongues of fire appeared and settled on each individual. The disciples were filled with the breath of God and began declaring his wonders in languages they had never learned.

They erupted into worship, and the joyful sound drew a large crowd, among them Jews from around the world. These Diaspora Jews were the descendants of those who had been driven into exile when Jerusalem fell to the Babylonians. To their surprise, they heard these Galileans speaking in languages they could understand. The curse of Babel was broken. All God's people were speaking with one voice, declaring his praises to the world. Jesus had prepared them; now his disciples are playing their part in God's story.

Peter reassures the crowd that they are not drunk, but—as the prophets promised—the Holy Spirit has been poured out. The last days have begun, and God is restoring Israel. He has established a new covenant with his people. He is fulfilling his ancient promise that he would give his people a new heart and put a new spirit in them; that he would remove their heart of stone and give them a heart of flesh (Ezekiel 36:26).

Peter challenged Israel to repent or face God's judgment. He told them that anyone who called on the name of the Lord Jesus would be saved. They had crucified the Messiah, but his death had atoned for their sins. Now risen and exalted to the right hand of God, the Lord Jesus had poured out his Holy Spirit. In a city of around one hundred thousand residents and pilgrims, three thousand believed and were baptized, and added to the one hundred and twenty followers of Jesus. The church was born!

The church in Jerusalem was drawn from a city that included Jews and Jewish converts who were Parthians, Medes, and Elamites. In addition, there were residents of Mesopotamia, Judea, Cappadocia, Pontus, Asia, Phrygia, and Pamphylia. Egyptians, Libyans, Romans, Cretans, and Arabs were also represented. Many went home to proclaim their faith in Jesus the Messiah. Because of this, churches were planted in cities such as Rome without any evidence of apostolic involvement.

The Spirit is God's powerful presence, and so when the Spirit came, the church's mission could begin. Throughout Acts, every breakthrough in the spread of the gospel is the initiative of the Holy Spirit.[2] How does the Spirit enable disciples to play their part in God's story? Peter, filled with the Spirit, boldly declared the gospel before the same people who crucified Jesus (Acts 4:7–13). The Spirit filled persecuted believers as they prayed, and they spoke the Word of God with boldness (Acts 4:31–32). The young church chose leaders who were filled with the Holy Spirit: one of them, Stephen, by the power of the Holy Spirit faced a violent death with courage (Acts 7:55); when Philip took the gospel to the Samaritans, God poured out his Holy Spirit on them (Acts 8:14–17); and the Holy Spirit guided Philip to an Ethiopian royal official, who became one of the first Gentile believers. The gospel spread into new regions by the power of the Spirit, often through unnamed ordinary disciples, resulting in a growing number of disciples and churches (Acts 9:31; 11:19–21). This was the work of the Holy Spirit in the mission of the church.

At Pentecost, Peter told his listeners that the Spirit had been poured out on *all* people—sons and daughters, young men and old men, *all* God's servants, both men and women. The Spirit is no longer limited to a chosen few with a special task. The Spirit is given to all, for inspired, powerful witness to the Lord Jesus from Jerusalem to the ends of the earth—the whole inhabited world. As Acts shows, where the Word goes in the power of the Spirit, the fruit is always new disciples and churches.

The Holy Spirit was poured out upon prepared people. Jesus had trained these men and women to play their part in God's story. He chose unlikely individuals, and then he shaped them. He taught them how to follow him together on the road. He taught them how to make disciples, and he taught them through their failures. He taught them God's story from Genesis to Malachi. Then he told them to go to the nations. The same Spirit that came upon Jesus to launch his mission, came upon his disciples—then and today—to continue it.

The Holy Spirit is the power of God's presence, applying the work of Christ in us and through us. He shapes us to become like the Lord Jesus. The Spirit enables us to play our part in taking the story of salvation to the entire world.[3]

YOUR PART IN GOD'S STORY

1. What are you learning about God and his mission?

_____

_____

_____

_____

_____

_____

_____

2. How does God shape the people he calls?

_____

_____

_____

_____

_____

_____

_____

3. What is God saying to you about your part in his story?

_____

_____

_____

_____

_____

_____

_____

4. How will you think and act differently?

_____

_____

_____

_____

_____

_____

_____

*All the
believers used
to meet together
in Solomon's
Colonnade. No one
else dared join them,
even though they were
highly regarded by the
people. Nevertheless, more
and more men and women
believed in the Lord and were
added to their number.*

ACTS 5:12–14

28

THE FIRST CHURCH

Read ACTS 2:36−47

When Peter had finished his Pentecost message, the people cried, "What should we do?" Peter told them to repent and be immersed (baptized) in the name of Jesus for the forgiveness of their sins. It was the message Jesus had also taught them—repent and believe—but there was something new: Jesus is now at the center of the proclamation.

Repentance is on the basis of the message about Jesus, Messiah and Lord. The promised rule of God has been fulfilled in him. He alone can save us from the coming judgment.[1] Baptism is in Jesus' name. Forgiveness of sins is only through his death and resurrection. Salvation is found in no other name under heaven (Acts 4:12). The focus of the proclamation has shifted from the kingdom to the King.[2]

The one conversion experience (which includes repentance, baptism, forgiveness of sins, and the infilling of the Holy Spirit) leads to discipleship in community (Acts 2:38).[3] Pentecost is the birth of the new people of God, the remnant of Israel, the church. Like Israel at the Exodus, this is a people rescued from captivity to become a kingdom of priests and a holy nation, who will display God's glory to the world. The church emerges out of Israel to draw in the nations.

The church in Jerusalem became the model for all other churches. Luke describes their life as an example to follow.

They were devoted to the teaching of the apostles. The Twelve were the authoritative witnesses to the mission and teaching of Jesus, and their teaching is preserved in the New Testament. The church also read the Old Testament with eyes opened by Jesus to see how the promises of God were fulfilled in him. The disciples were *devoted* to the Word of God entrusted to the apostles—implying they didn't just hear but were willing to obey what they learned.

The church in Jerusalem shared their lives with one another. These disciples loved each other because Jesus first loved them. They were united by the same Holy Spirit. They met from house to house. They met in Solomon's Colonnade on the Temple Mount (Acts 5:12), fulfilling Jesus' declaration that the temple should be a house of prayer (Luke 19:45–46).

They broke bread together. The breaking of bread refers to ordinary shared meals in homes and at the temple courts. Within those meals, they shared the Lord's Supper and remembered Jesus' death on the cross for the forgiveness of sins, as Jesus had commanded them to do (Luke 22:14–22).[4]

This church was born, and continued to grow, in prayer and worship. In homes and throughout the temple courts, they continued to praise God with glad and sincere hearts. They prayed with joy because God was present. They prayed when selecting leaders (Acts 1:24–25). They prayed for healing (Acts 3:6). They prayed when they were persecuted (Acts 4:23–31). Leaders devoted themselves to prayer (Acts 6:4). They prayed for new believers to receive the Holy Spirit (Acts 8:15).

The early church experienced the presence and power of the Holy Spirit in tangible ways. They were filled with awe. Signs and wonders accompanied the spreading of the Word. The Spirit worked in the life of the church to bring diverse people groups into the blessings of the kingdom—Samaritans, an Ethiopian, a Roman centurion and his family and friends, God-fearing Gentiles, and pagans.

The believers were in the habit of selling property and possessions to give money to those in need. Wealthier believers, such as Joseph Barnabas, were not compelled to sell their property, but they chose to give as needs arose within the community (Acts 4:37; 5:1–11).

As the believers experienced God's presence, God added to their number every day. The movement grew and multiplied, not just conversions but baptized disciples following Jesus together. Soon, the disciples had filled Jerusalem with their teaching (Acts 5:28). The Word of God spread, the number of disciples increased rapidly, and a large number of priests became obedient to the faith (Acts 6:7). The movement spread from Jerusalem, and churches were planted in the cities and villages of Judea, Galilee, and Samaria (Acts 9:31).

What began as a fearful and fractured band of disciples became a missionary movement. Despite persecution, and sometimes *because* of persecution (Acts 8:1), the first church became a multiplying movement of churches crossing ethnic, cultural, and religious barriers, from Jerusalem to the ends of the earth—as Jesus had promised. Luke wants us to watch and learn from the church in Jerusalem; they modeled how a community of disciples can play its part in God's story.[5]

YOUR PART IN GOD'S STORY

1. What are you learning about God and his mission?

_____

_____

_____

_____

_____

_____

2. How does God shape the people he calls?

_____

_____

_____

_____

_____

_____

_____

3. What is God saying to you about your part in his story?

_____

_____

_____

_____

_____

_____

_____

4. How will you think and act differently?

_____

_____

_____

_____

_____

_____

_____

Why do the nations rage and the peoples plot in vain?

ACTS 4:25

29

PERSECUTION AND POWER

Read ACTS 4:1—31

As the gospel filled Jerusalem, it was inevitable there would be trouble. It began when Peter and John went to the temple at the hour of prayer and healed a lame beggar in Jesus' name. The man rose to his feet and began walking and jumping and praising God. News spread throughout the city, and a crowd gathered around them at Solomon's Colonnade. Peter seized the opportunity and preached. Thousands believed.

A group called the Sadducees controlled the temple, the priesthood, and the ruling Jewish council (the Sanhedrin). Their power came from their alliance with Rome. In his message, Peter accused Jerusalem's ruling elite of complicity in the death of Jesus—the Messiah and author of life. Peter's boldness was costly; the Sadducees arrested Peter and John, and threw them in jail.

The next morning, the Sanhedrin—the same body that had condemned Jesus to death—met to consider the matter. They could not deny that a man had been healed, and Peter and John refused to be silenced, declaring their obedience to God, not man. Afraid of the people, who were all praising God, the Sanhedrin threatened the apostles but released them.

Peter and John were free. Not long ago, when Jesus was arrested, these same men had fled in the face of danger. The same authorities now had them in their sights. Perhaps Peter and John were tempted to leave Jerusalem and lie low for a while back in Galilee. Instead, they boldly declared that they couldn't help but speak. Jesus had captured their hearts. The Holy Spirit had made them bold. They chose to obey Jesus and play their part in God's story, regardless of the consequences.

Instead of running from danger, they sought out the believers and gave a full report. When they'd finished, the room erupted into prayer. Luke shows us how a movement responds to persecution. Their prayer began by placing the threat in the context of who God is and how he is at work to fulfil his purposes. They turned to Psalm 2 and prayed the Scriptures. God is the Sovereign Lord who made the heavens, the earth, and the sea—and everything in them. He rules over the world he has made. He rules over history. Why should they fear men?

They took David's words in the psalm to be the words of God, inspired by the Holy Spirit. Herod and Pilate were just like the rulers who opposed God and his king in David's day. These men can only do what God allows. The believers will not give these rulers a place only God can occupy. The battle is the Lord's. "The One enthroned in heaven laughs!" (Psalm 2:4).

In their prayer, these harassed believers have not asked God for anything. In a dangerous world, they remembered who God is and placed themselves in his care. Without telling God what to do, they asked him to take note of the threats made against them. God will take note, and he will bring these rulers to account.

Now it was time for the believers to bring their needs to God. Did they ask for protection, safety, and peace? No. Just one request—help us speak your Word with *boldness*. In the face of persecution, they want to be bold. That is how a movement prays when it's in trouble. Their prayer reveals their surrender. They are ready to play their part in God's story. They ask for boldness—confidence, openness, freedom—as they keep speaking God's Word. This boldness is not natural; it is a gift from God.

They also ask God to stretch out his hand to heal and perform signs and wonders. They could have asked for miracles of judgment upon their oppressors; instead, they ask for miracles of mercy.[1] The signs they seek are in Jesus' name, and they confirm the message about him.

This is a movement facing a crisis, responding in prayer. They remembered who God is, and they asked for boldness so that the gospel would go out in power. These believers knew they were praying themselves into greater trouble *and* a greater harvest.

God answered, and the house was shaken. Similar to Pentecost, they were *all* filled with the Holy Spirit, and they *all* spoke the Word of God boldly—not just the apostles, but *all* the believers. In Acts, the Word goes out through leaders and ordinary people wherever they go.[2]

This will not be the last time the movement is threatened with violence. Messengers are beaten, arrested, jailed, put on trial, and executed. Yet somehow the Word continued to grow, spread, and multiply. At the forefront were ordinary people whose lives had been transformed by the Word and the Spirit. The gospel went out, disciples were made, and churches were planted in Jerusalem, Judea, Samaria, and to the ends of the earth.

YOUR PART IN GOD'S STORY

1. What are you learning about God and his mission?

_____

_____

_____

_____

_____

_____

2. How does God shape the people he calls?

_____

_____

_____

_____

_____

_____

_____

3. What is God saying to you about your part in his story?

_____

_____

_____

_____

_____

_____

_____

4. How will you think and act differently?

_____

_____

_____

_____

_____

_____

_____

I am Jesus,
whom you are
persecuting.

ACTS 9:5

30

EATING DUST ON THE DAMASCUS ROAD

Read ACTS 7:54–8:3; 9:1–22

Stephen was the first person to die for his faith in Jesus. He was stoned to death by an enraged mob around AD 31/32.[1] Before the final blow struck, Stephen fell to his knees and, like Jesus, prayed that God would forgive his attackers. As Stephen is dying, Luke turns his spotlight for a moment on a young man who is watching on. For Saul this was just the beginning. He is about to launch a campaign to destroy this movement of Jesus' followers wherever he can find them.

When we hear of Saul again, he is going from house to house, arresting and imprisoning men and women. Driven by a murderous rage, Saul became a leading figure in a great persecution that broke out in Jerusalem.

Saul went to the High Priest Caiaphas (the one who had condemned Jesus) for authority to hunt down followers of Jesus who had fled north to Damascus.

Damascus was the prosperous center of the Roman province of Syria on the main trade route between North Africa and Mesopotamia. It was also home to a large Jewish community and a natural refuge for Jewish Christians fleeing persecution in Jerusalem.[2]

When he got to Damascus, Saul intended to introduce himself to the local authorities, gather names and addresses of followers of Jesus, arrest them and return them to Jerusalem under guard.[3]

As he approached the city, there was a blinding light, and Saul was thrown to the ground. He heard the words, "Saul, Saul, why do you persecute me?" Saul thought he was serving God, but he had been fighting against God, persecuting God's people, and in doing so, persecuting Israel's Messiah.

The risen Lord intervened to protect his church and transform Saul into the pioneer of a movement that would reach the nations.[4] Jesus, who began this movement, continued to lead it.

Helpless, blinded by the glory of the risen Messiah, and led by the hand, Saul stumbled into Damascus. It was a very different arrival than he had planned. For three days he sat in darkness and did not eat or drink. Humbled, he waited for God to make the next move.

God sent a disciple called Ananias to speak to Paul. Despite a vision from God, Ananias was reluctant to go, unconvinced it was safe to contact this enemy of God's people. The Lord ended the discussion with the command to "Go!" and Ananias obeyed.

He was sent to a house on Straight Street, the main east-west road through Damascus, which is still there today. When he arrived, Ananias addressed Saul as *brother*. Saul received a prophetic word through Ananias, as well as his healing, and the filling of the Holy Spirit. Paul submitted to baptism, and with that, the great persecutor of Jesus of Nazareth became his humble servant.

What irony when Ananias introduced Saul as a brother to the disciples in Damascus, the very people whom Saul had come to arrest!

The story of Paul's conversion is so important that Luke tells it three times.[5] From the accounts, we can see how God called Paul and shaped him to play a part in his story.

The Lord intervened and chose Paul, not by merit but by grace. Paul was commissioned as a witness to Jews and Gentiles to what he had seen and heard. He will face rejection and experience suffering, but God will rescue him. Paul will bring light where there is darkness. He will deliver people from the power of Satan to God. Paul will preach repentance and faith, resulting in the forgiveness of sins and inclusion among God's people.[6] This is Paul's mission because it is God's mission.

God's call came as a gift that cost everything. Paul answered with faith and obedience. He began preaching fearlessly in the synagogues of Damascus, proclaiming that Jesus is the Son of God (Acts 9:20–28). Jesus told Ananias, "I will show him [Paul] how much he must suffer for my name." Those words were soon fulfilled. Saul the persecutor became Paul the persecuted and suffered like his Lord.[7]

Before we can play our part in God's story, we must first experience his love and forgiveness. We have nothing to offer God except our need. We have nothing to add except our surrender. Our service is a gift to the one who gave us life.

Paul was in no doubt about the nature of his mission. It would not be easy, but it was clear. The risen Lord sent him to deliver people from the power of Satan by calling them to repentance and faith, resulting in forgiveness and inclusion among God's people. Wherever Paul went, the gospel went with him, and the fruit of his ministry is evidenced in new disciples and churches to the glory of God.

YOUR PART IN GOD'S STORY

1. What are you learning about God and his mission?

_____

_____

_____

_____

_____

_____

_____

2. How does God shape the people he calls?

_____

_____

_____

_____

_____

_____

_____

_____

3. What is God saying to you about your part in his story?

_____

_____

_____

_____

_____

_____

_____

_____

4. How will you think and act differently?

_____

_____

_____

_____

_____

_____

_____

While they were worshiping the Lord and fasting, the Holy Spirit said, "Set apart for me Barnabas and Saul for the work to which I have called them."

ACTS 13:2

31

THE WORK

Read ACTS 13–14

In the spring of AD 45, prophets and teachers from the church at Antioch in Syria were worshiping, fasting, and praying when the Holy Spirit spoke.[1] Antioch was the first church with a significant mix of Jews and Gentiles. It was therefore fitting that the Spirit would call two of its leaders to launch a mission to Gentiles living in the eastern half of the Roman Empire. This campaign was initiated, led, and sustained by God's powerful presence.

Paul and Barnabas had a broad vision. They sailed to Cyprus, then went throughout the island until they reached Paphos. They then climbed the steep roads up the rugged Taurus Mountains to reach Pisidian Antioch. From there, the Word of the Lord spread throughout the region.[2] They walked on to Iconium, Lystra, and Derbe. In Derbe, the whole city heard the gospel, and a large number of disciples were won. Finally, they circled back to the cities in which they had faced opposition.[3] There was an easier road home, but they wanted to go back and strengthen the disciples and churches and appoint local leaders.[4] Then they could say they had completed the work; they had played their part in God's mission.

In each place, if there was a Jewish synagogue, Paul and Barnabas went there first to connect with people and to preach and teach. This had been Jesus' priority, and it continued to be a priority for Paul. There were also good strategic reasons to go to the Jews first. Paul and Barnabas were Jews from the Diaspora, outside Israel. These were the people with whom they had religious, linguistic, cultural, and relational ties. In the synagogue, they also met God-fearing Gentiles who were closely connected with pagan Gentiles in the community. This way the gospel spread through preexisting relationships.

The content of the good news centered on the life, death, resurrection, and exaltation of Jesus as Savior and Lord. In each place, they proclaimed the Word and tailored their message to their listeners.[5] Luke provides examples of their preaching to both Jews and to pagan Gentiles.[6] In Acts, the Word grows in power, spreads, and multiplies. Once it took root, the new disciples spread the gospel beyond the cities to whole regions.

When the gospel was met by faith, Paul and Barnabas founded communities of Jesus' disciples. The goal of their mission was healthy churches. Often driven out of a city, Paul and Barnabas risked their safety by returning, once the trouble had died down, so they could strengthen the disciples and churches and appoint elders. They taught the disciples to expect persecution, reminding them they must go through many hardships to enter God's kingdom. Before they left, they committed the believers to the Lord, confident that the new churches could trust God to bring them to maturity.

John Mark accompanied Paul and Barnabas. Though John Mark left prematurely, his involvement in the mission shows the apostles' intention to train and multiply workers as they went. Eventually Paul returned to Lystra with Silas and recruited Timothy to his team (Acts 16:3). Paul was in the habit of recruiting workers to his missionary band from the churches he planted (Acts 20:4). The apostles did not settle down to become long-term pastors. In every place, they formed disciples into self-governing, self-sustaining churches, with local leaders who could reach their region in depth.

Their mission put Paul and Barnabas in conflict with the powers of evil and their representatives.[7] Their first confrontation was in Cyprus with a sorcerer and false prophet. Satan was also at work in the violence of their opponents. They weren't persecuted everywhere, but when it came, their first response was boldness—they remained confident and open in proclaiming the gospel. If the opposition grew to a dangerous level, they left for the next city. Later, they returned to strengthen the disciples and churches.

At the beginning of the journey, the Spirit set Paul and Barnabas aside for the work. By the end of the journey, they had finished the job; they had completed the work the Holy Spirit gave them. That work involved pioneer evangelism, forming new disciples into churches, strengthening them, and appointing local leaders. The churches became partners in the mission by reaching out to their region and providing workers for Paul as he pushed into new fields.

God had opened the door of faith to the Gentiles. There were now disciples and churches in cities, and through them the Word was spreading throughout the regions. Acts is the story of how the risen Lord continued his mission through his disciples in the power of the Spirit, from Jerusalem to the ends of the earth.

YOUR PART IN GOD'S STORY

1. What are you learning about God and his mission?

_____

_____

_____

_____

_____

_____

2. How does God shape the people he calls?

_____

_____

_____

_____

_____

_____

3. What is God saying to you about your part in his story?

_____

_____

_____

_____

_____

_____

_____

4. How will you think and act differently?

_____

_____

_____

_____

_____

_____

_____

*Stand firm in
the one Spirit,
striving together
as one for the faith
of the gospel without
being frightened in any
way by those who oppose
you.*

PHILIPPIANS 1:27–28

32

TO LIVE IS CHRIST,
TO DIE IS GAIN

Read PHILIPPIANS 1:12–29

Philippi was a key city in the Roman province of Macedonia (northern Greece). It was a Roman colony made up of Greeks and Romans. Paul first arrived in Philippi in AD 49.[1] There he preached the gospel and started a church in the home of a wealthy merchant named Lydia (Acts 16:11–40).

Twelve years later, Paul was in Rome as a prisoner awaiting trial for his life before Emperor Nero. For two years he was allowed to stay in rented accommodation, while chained to a soldier night and day.[2] It's likely that this is when Paul wrote his letter to the Philippians.[3]

Paul told the Philippian church that he was full of joy as he prayed for them. They had partnered with him in the spread of the gospel since the day they first believed, and played their part in the mission by praying for him and by proclaiming the good news themselves.[4] At the end of the letter, Paul thanked them again for their partnership, this time for their giving towards his work in other fields.

Paul wrote to them because the church was suffering. They were threatened by persecution and by division. Drawing on his current experience, Paul encouraged the Philippians to remain faithful, for his sufferings had advanced the gospel. He was in chains, and on trial for his life, but the gospel still went out. The knowledge of Christ was spreading throughout the elite Praetorian Guards, charged with the emperor's protection. In addition, there were now believers in Caesar's own household, the body responsible for running the empire.[5] Finally, because of Paul's example, most of the believers in Rome had become confident in the Lord and were proclaiming the gospel without fear.

Paul knew that some in Rome proclaimed Christ from mixed motives. They weren't interested in partnership with him but saw themselves as rivals to his mission. But Paul wasn't worried. What mattered to him was that the gospel was getting out. Like Paul, the Philippians were facing persecution and threatened with disunity. He wanted them to be united as they contended for the gospel.

Christ was working in Paul's imprisonment for the advance of the gospel at the center of the empire.[6] In the same way, Christ was at work among the Philippians for the spread of the gospel, even in their suffering. Paul wanted them to imitate him, and the Christians in Rome, by sharing the good news, despite the opposition.[7] He wanted the churches in Rome and Philippi to play their part with him in God's mission.

Paul wasn't ashamed or frustrated by his imprisonment; he rejoiced in it! He knew that as the believers prayed for him, the Spirit of Christ was working and could rescue him. He was ready to be freed. He was also ready to be condemned and executed. What mattered to Paul was that Christ was proclaimed. Paul was focused on playing his part in God's story.

To live is Christ, to die is gain.

YOUR PART IN GOD'S STORY

1. What are you learning about God and his mission?

_____

_____

_____

_____

_____

_____

2. How does God shape the people he calls?

_____

_____

_____

_____

_____

_____

_____

3. What is God saying to you about your part in his story?

_____

_____

_____

_____

_____

_____

_____

4. How will you think and act differently?

_____

_____

_____

_____

_____

_____

_____

*I planted the
seed, Apollos
watered it, but
God has been
making it grow.*

I CORINTHIANS 3:6

33

WHAT IS APOLLOS?
AND WHAT IS PAUL?

Read | CORINTHIANS 3:5—17

Paul arrived in Corinth from Athens early in AD 50.[1] Corinth was the lead city of the Roman province of Achaia in southern Greece. There, Paul built a team with Aquila and Priscilla, and after Timothy and Silas arrived, he devoted himself full-time to preaching the gospel. His mission to the city of eighty thousand lasted eighteen months, and many Jews and Gentiles were converted despite opposition. The fruit of the mission was new disciples gathered in new churches throughout the city and the province of Achaia.[2] In this way, Paul and his team played their part in God's story.

A few years later, the relationship between Paul and the church had deteriorated. The church were now evaluating leaders according to human wisdom and were forming factions. Paul wrote to explain his role as the church's founder and that of other leaders who followed him.

He begins here with an example from farming. Paul and his coworkers are servants in God's field. They follow Jesus who came as a Servant.[3] The cross was both their message and their ministry model.

It is God's field, and he has given different jobs to each worker. Each person has a part in his story. Paul planted, Apollos watered, but God gave the growth. Everything is

God's—the land, the workers, and the growth of crops. Without God's work to bring people to faith and cause them to grow in Christ, there would be no church.[4] Workers come and go, and they make their contribution, but the field is the Lord's; the fruit is his doing. The church does not belong to the apostle or to its local leaders or even to its people. It is God's church and his mission.

Paul moves the imagery from a farm to a construction site. Paul is called to establish churches. He is a skilled master builder who lays the foundation. He is a hands-on building supervisor who gets the job done.[5]

Paul was a pioneer, but his work wasn't done when someone was converted. He proclaimed the gospel, made disciples, formed new disciples into churches, and strengthened those churches. That is the core missionary task—from pioneering in unreached fields to reproducing disciples and churches.

The message of the crucified and risen Christ is the foundation of the church. That message determines the life of the church. It is possible to build on another basis, but it won't be a church. The world's wisdom does not compare to the power of Christ crucified in the establishment and growth of the churches. Leaders are responsible to God for the part they play and the way they build. Those who build upon a foundation are wise to stay within its limits. If a builder changes the specifications, the building will not stand when it is tested, and poor workmanship will be exposed.

A builder must use the right materials. Gold, silver, precious stones, and marble will survive a fire; other materials, such as wood, hay, and straw will not.[6] Leaders who compromise the message of the crucified and risen Savior will see their work destroyed in the last judgment. They will be like someone running through the flames of a badly built house. They may escape, but their work will be lost.

These Corinthians were former pagans, who were used to visiting temples and shrines where their gods lived. The word Paul uses for temple refers to the most holy place within the temple.[7] As Paul and others established disciples in church communities, they were building God's holy temple on earth, and the Spirit dwelt among them.

God's ancient promises to dwell with his people were being fulfilled as Paul planted churches along the major routes of the Roman Empire. These gathered communities, with all their issues, were temples of the living God, his dwelling place on earth. As such, they had a part to play in God's mission.

Paul finished with a solemn warning: if anyone destroys God's temple, God will destroy them. The Corinthians found many ways to destroy a church—factions, the wisdom of the world, sexual immorality, legalism.

A church that is no longer built on Christ crucified is no longer a church. His judgment will come, because his temple is sacred. Paul was challenging the Corinthians to become what, by God's grace they were: God's holy temple in Corinth.[8] Only then could they play their part in God's story.

Leaders have a part to play; churches have a part to play. But it is God who shapes them for his mission.

YOUR PART IN GOD'S STORY

1. What are you learning about God and his mission?

_____

_____

_____

_____

_____

_____

2. How does God shape the people he calls?

_____

_____

_____

_____

_____

_____

_____

3. What is God saying to you about your part in his story?

_____

_____

_____

_____

_____

_____

_____

4. How will you think and act differently?

_____

_____

_____

_____

_____

_____

_____

*He said to
me, "My grace
is sufficient for
you, for my power
is made perfect in
weakness." Therefore
I will boast all the
more gladly about my
weaknesses, so that Christ's
power may rest on me.*

2 CORINTHIANS 12:9

34

THE POWER OF WEAKNESS

Read 2 CORINTHIANS 4:1–18

Paul's authority as an apostle was under attack: the Corinthians saw him as weak. Letters and messengers have gone back and forth, and Paul has made an urgent and painful visit to Corinth, followed up by a tearful letter (2 Corinthians 2:1–4).

Paul shared in the sufferings of Christ. His sufferings were so great that Paul despaired of life itself. The experience taught him to rely on God, who raises the dead. The secret to playing his part in God's story was discovering God's power in his weakness.

As a former persecutor of God's church, Paul knows he has this ministry by God's mercy, so he doesn't lose heart. He doesn't need to manipulate people through cunning and deception. He will not distort God's Word to impress his listeners.[1] Unlike others, who are "peddlers" of God's Word, he will not dilute the gospel message to please his audience (2 Corinthians 2:17).

Paul presents the gospel plainly, and if the gospel is hidden, it is not because of ineffective communication. The minds of those who reject the message have been blinded by the god of this age. Satan has usurped God's authority, and through humanity's rebellion, claimed power over this world. Paul's mind was once blinded by the god of this age when he persecuted the church. Then he saw the glory of God in the face of Jesus, who is the image of God.[2] The glory of God is revealed in the crucified and risen Lord. This is Paul's message.

The weakness of the messenger reveals the treasure we contain. Clay pots are cheap, easily broken, and thrown away. We are the clay pots that contain the gospel, so that the power of God is revealed in our weakness. The splendor of God is revealed in the message, not the messenger.

Paul is hard-pressed, not crushed; perplexed, not in despair; persecuted, not abandoned; struck down, not destroyed. As disciples of Jesus, we suffer the same fate as our Lord, who came to serve and give his life as a ransom. Yet, at the same time, we also know the power of his resurrection. As we share in both the suffering and power of Jesus, God shapes us to play our part in his story.

Paul suffered because, like Jesus, he did not abandon God's mission. Suffering is not an end in itself. We share in the death of Jesus so that the life of Jesus will be revealed in us. Paul learned to delight in his weaknesses, in insults, in hardships, in persecutions, in difficulties. The outcome was that Christ's power rested on him. "For when I am weak, then I am strong" (2 Corinthians 12:10). For Paul, knowing Christ meant to know both the power of his resurrection and the fellowship of his sufferings (Philippians 3:10).

The center of Paul's mission is the cross of Christ. Paul proclaimed that truth with both his words and his life. Others were confident in their own power. Paul calls them "super-apostles" (2 Corinthians 11:5). The spotlight was on them, not on the glory of God in the face of Christ crucified.

Paul knows one day the struggle will be over. The One who raised Jesus from the dead will also raise Paul and present him to Jesus, together with the disciples and churches that are the fruit of his ministry. They are his reward in Christ.[3] Paul serves so that *they* can experience the grace of God. Through them, grace will spread to more and more people, who will overflow with thankfulness, bringing glory to God. This is what motivates Paul: the joy of God's grace reaching more and more people.

Suffering cannot defeat the purposes of God. Outwardly, Paul is wasting away every day. Inwardly, he is being renewed daily by the life of Christ. His troubles are light and momentary compared to the eternal weight of glory. Suffering is real but temporary; the age to come is eternal.[4]

Trouble marked the whole of Paul's missionary career. From the beginning, his apostolic call was also a call to suffer (Acts 9:16). As he completed his mission to Ephesus, the Spirit warned him that prison and hardship awaited him in every city (Acts 20:23).

Paul was moved by his experience of God in hard places. When he was distressed, he felt God's comfort. When he was weak, he experienced the power that raised Jesus from the dead. When he felt under the sentence of death, God raised him up. When his troubles drove him to despair, he set his hope on God. He discovered God in hard places.

That's how God shapes those who want to play their part in his story.

YOUR PART IN GOD'S STORY

1. What are you learning about God and his mission?

_____

_____

_____

_____

_____

_____

2. How does God shape the people he calls?

_____

_____

_____

_____

_____

_____

_____

3. What is God saying to you about your part in his story?

_____

_____

_____

_____

_____

_____

_____

4. How will you think and act differently?

_____

_____

_____

_____

_____

_____

_____

*The God of
peace will soon
crush Satan under
your feet.*

ROMANS 16:20

35

THE FIGHT

Read EPHESIANS 6:10–20

From AD 52–54, Paul was in Ephesus, the center of the worship of Artemis, goddess of the underworld. Artemis' temple in the city was one of the Seven Wonders of the ancient world. The Ephesians were devoted to Artemis, as well as to their practice of magic. Despite spiritual opposition, which erupted in violence, Paul left behind a network of churches in the city and throughout Asia Minor (modern Turkey).[1]

A few years later, Paul wrote to the churches from Rome where he was under house arrest, awaiting trial.[2] He wanted to remind them of who they are in Christ. They are blessed by the Father, redeemed by the blood of Christ, sealed with the Holy Spirit. The same power—that raised Jesus and seated him at God's right hand above all rule and authority, power, dominion, and every name—is available to those who believe. Paul wanted to help them deal with the spiritual forces behind the gods they once worshiped and the spirits they once feared.

In this passage, Paul addresses the spiritual battle that rages around every disciple playing their part in God's mission. The scene is a military camp. Soldiers are preparing to go into battle. Piece by piece, they are putting on their armor, preparing for a life-and-death struggle. Like a commanding officer challenging his troops to "Be strong!" as they prepare to fight, Paul urges the Ephesians to be strong in the Lord and in his mighty power. This strength is a gift from God, which comes to those who are united with Christ in his death and resurrection and are therefore seated with him in heavenly places (Ephesians 2:6).

Paul is being held captive by the power of Rome, but the struggle is not against flesh and blood. Sin has opened the door to evil forces that are at work in the world. There are powerful spiritual beings that attack believers, tempting them to sin or diverting them from God's purposes.[3]

Paul doesn't satisfy our curiosity and unpack what he means by these rulers, authorities, powers, and spiritual forces. Instead, his focus is on how we stand firm and how we win victory. We stand together by resisting the assault. We win victory by bringing the good news to the captives.[4]

Paul describes our fight with the devil as a wrestle. It's hand-to-hand combat. For this, we need the belt of truth around our waist. We must hold to the truth of who we are in Christ and take that truth to the world. As we do, we are protected by the breastplate of righteousness. The breastplate covers the chest and protects vital organs from arrows, spears, and sword thrusts. We are to clothe ourselves in God's righteousness in Christ.

Next comes our footwear, essential for long marches and for grip in the heat of battle. We must stand firm in the fight, announcing the victory of Jesus, who has won peace through his death. Only the gospel can rescue the captives from the kingdom of darkness.

Now comes the shield; not a small round one used in single combat, but a door-shaped Roman shield, protecting every part of the body. Designed for an army, marching shoulder-to-shoulder, these shields would lock together to form an impenetrable wall. Paul expects us to go into battle as a united army, protected by our faith in the promises of God. In the garden, the Serpent picked off the woman and the man one by one. They did not trust God's Word, and Satan took them captive. The Roman shield had leather stretched over it and was soaked in water, designed specifically to protect a soldier from arrows that were dipped in tar, set alight, then fired. Faith in the character and promises of God is our one defense against every flaming arrow the enemy sends our way.

A Roman soldier's helmet was made of bronze, which protected the head, along with two sidepieces, which protected the face. When Yahweh goes into battle against his enemies, he wears the helmet of salvation (Isaiah 59:17). The helmet of salvation is a gift to us from our Warrior King. We were dead in our sins, under the rule of darkness, deserving the wrath of God, but because of his great love, he made us alive in Christ.[5] So we march into battle, heads held high.

In the press of battle, there was no room to swing a broadsword. Roman armies conquered the world with their short swords. The sword is the Word of God—written and proclaimed, placed in our hands by the Holy Spirit.

In the wilderness, Jesus repelled Satan with the sword of the Spirit. We are to take hold of the Word of God and proclaim it in the power of the Spirit.[6] "The Word of God and the work of the Spirit are the means by which the people of God step out in defiance of Satan and rob his domain."[7]

Finally, prayer is the secret to how we use our armor and weapons in battle.[8] Notice the repetition of *all/always*. We are to pray in the Spirit on *all* occasions with *all* kinds of prayers and requests and to *always* keep on praying for *all* the Lord's people. In this battle, we stand by praying in the Spirit—guided, inspired, sustained by the Spirit, who helps us in our weakness and prays for us.[9] Prayer is an important way we play our part in God's story.

Paul asks for prayer for himself as he wields the sword of the Spirit. Paul doesn't ask for freedom from prison; he asks for fearlessness. He wants to stand in chains before Emperor Nero and proclaim the good news.

YOUR PART IN GOD'S STORY

1. What are you learning about God and his mission?

_____

_____

_____

_____

_____

_____

2. How does God shape the people he calls?

_____

_____

_____

_____

_____

_____

3. What is God saying to you about your part in his story?

_____

_____

_____

_____

_____

_____

_____

4. How will you think and act differently?

_____

_____

_____

_____

_____

_____

_____

*You know how
I lived the whole
time I was with
you.*

ACTS 20:18

36

LOOKING BACK

Read ACTS 20:17—38

With his ship moored at the harbor in Miletus, Paul sent a message to the elders of the churches in and around Ephesus to meet him. Paul had come to say goodbye. After Jerusalem, he was headed to Rome and then further west to Spain. His message to the Ephesian elders gave Paul a chance to reflect on his missionary task.

Between AD 45–57, Paul and his coworkers founded churches in the Roman provinces of Syria-Cilicia, Cyprus, Galatia, Macedonia, Achaia, and Asia Minor.[1] His mission to the eastern half of the Roman Empire was complete. Paul was pressing on to make it to Jerusalem by Pentecost.

All the roads of Asia Minor converged on Ephesus, making it the hub of the region. While Paul was in Ephesus, the gospel went out to the whole province, and churches were planted in the neighboring cities of Laodicea, Hierapolis, and Colossae.[2]

Paul cast a broad net. He sought out observant Jews, Gentile God-fearers, and pagan Greeks. Paul encountered people in public places, such as synagogues, the market place at the city center, and public buildings. He went from house to house, as new converts and their friends and family gathered to hear more.

To both Jews and Greeks, Paul declared that they must turn to God in repentance and have faith in our Lord Jesus.

Paul held nothing back. He spoke freely and openly. He declared that all must repent, they must turn away from their sin, and serve the living and true God on God's own terms.[3]

Paul knew his part in God's mission. Wherever he went, he made disciples and started and strengthened churches. He stayed in Ephesus for almost three years, ensuring the new believers understood and lived out the implications of the gospel in their lives. Paul taught them the whole will of God revealed in Jesus Christ, and night and day with tears, he warned each disciple to remain faithful. He shared the Word, and he shared his life. As he spoke, Paul reminded the elders of his tears, his humility, his hard work to support himself, his courage in persecution, boldness in proclamation, obedience to the Spirit, faithfulness to the task, and freedom in generosity. He had loved them.

The fruit of Paul's mission was God's church, which God bought with his own blood. These leaders are shepherds of God's church, appointed by the Holy Spirit. The churches do not belong to them, for they have been purchased by the sacrificial death of Christ. The churches belong to God and are in his care.[4]

After Paul goes, these local leaders will face fierce opposition from outside and from within, just as Paul had. The enemy will send savage wolves among the sheep. They must now deal with it, for Paul has played his part. His job is done. The Word had gone out to the whole of Asia Minor, bearing the fruit of new disciples and churches. Paul has raised up local leaders out of that harvest; now they must enter the fight as Paul moves on to new fields. He leaves behind the memory of his example and the confidence that the risen Lord is active in the church through his living Word and the Holy Spirit.

As Paul speaks to the elders of the Ephesian church, seven men watch and listen.[5] They are Paul's travelling companions, who came from the churches he started, the fruit of his ministry throughout the Eastern Empire. They are observing and learning from an apostolic pioneer who has finished his assignment. They're catching his heart.

At the heart of God's mission, through Paul and his co-workers, is the gospel, which goes out in the power of the Spirit and finds faith. Churches have sprung up throughout Ephesus and the whole of Asia Minor. They are ready to stand on their own two feet and fight their own battles. They have the memory of Paul's example; they have the Word and the Spirit; they have the leaders Paul has trained. They can continue the work. Paul's job is done.

Compelled by the Spirit, Paul is going to Jerusalem, where the Spirit has warned him he will face prison and hardship. He will finish the race and complete the task Jesus has given him—the task of testifying to the good news of God's grace.

The elders gather around him. They kneel, they pray, and they weep, for they will never see Paul again.

YOUR PART IN GOD'S STORY

1. What are you learning about God and his mission?

_____

_____

_____

_____

_____

_____

2. How does God shape the people he calls?

_____

_____

_____

_____

_____

_____

_____

3. What is God saying to you about your part in his story?

_____

_____

_____

_____

_____

_____

_____

4. How will you think and act differently?

_____

_____

_____

_____

_____

_____

_____

For I am not ashamed of the gospel, because it is the power of God that brings salvation to everyone who believes.

ROMANS 1:16

37

I AM NOT ASHAMED

Read ROMANS 1:16—32; 3:21—26

Paul wrote to the churches in Rome to introduce himself and the gospel he proclaimed, seeking their partnership in the mission (Romans 15:4). His work in the eastern Mediterranean was finished; there were now churches in major cities in an arc all the way from Jerusalem to the Roman province Illyricum on the east coast of the Adriatic Sea. As an apostle, he preached where Christ was not yet known, and so Paul headed west to Spain.

Paul explains that the wrath of God is at work. God's wrath is his settled, active opposition to everything that is evil.[1] God is not indifferent to evil—there will be a final judgment, and his wrath is at work in the world today. When his love will not lead us to repentance, God disciplines us because of his love for us.[2]

Paul goes on to say that the world is without excuse. God has made himself known through the world he created. What light we have, we have ignored. The world has turned from the knowledge of God to gods of their own making. They worship the creation, not the Creator. They live in darkness.[3]

When we rebel against him, God's judgment comes in an unexpected form. Paul makes it clear that God gives us over to our own desires, whether that be sexual immorality, wickedness, greed, depravity, envy, murder, deceit, hatred, or anything else. Such people, Paul says, have no understanding, no faithfulness, no love or mercy. God hands us over to the consequences of our rebellion, so we will look to him for mercy.

God will not pretend that our sin does not matter; to do so would be to destroy his image in us. Until we face this sad reality, we will not understand the importance of the gospel or be motivated to proclaim it.[4]

Paul starts Romans 3:21 with: *But now.* This simple phrase says it all. We are all bound by the power of sin and rightly deserve God's judgment, *but now* God has revealed his righteousness. Out of his great love, he has made a way to bring us into right relationship with himself.[5] The Old Testament law revealed how his people should live, but in a fallen world the law could never save. Made in the image of God, the standard has always been the glory of God. We were made to be like Christ, and that was lost. That's what it means to fall short of the glory of God.

Salvation has always been through faith, trusting God's promises of mercy and forgiveness. This was achieved by Christ's violent death: God presented Christ as a sacrifice of atonement and passed over our sins. Forgiveness cost God everything. No one can accuse him of injustice. God's righteousness is now available through faith in Christ to everyone who believes, and is only made possible through God's holy love revealed in the cross. God does what is right: his wrath judges sin; his love forgives sinners. We walk free.

This is what Jesus meant when he said, "Whoever hears my word and believes him who sent me has eternal life and will not be judged but has crossed over from death to life" (John 5:24). He is the Good Shepherd who lays down his life for the sheep (John 10:11). He is the Son of Man who was lifted up on a cross and draws all people to himself (John 12:32).

Paul knows the terrible plight humanity faces. He knows the holy love of God revealed in the death and resurrection of Jesus. He knows everyone who calls on the name of Jesus will be saved. How could he not go? How could he stay silent? Like Jesus, Paul was motivated by God's love for lost and broken people.

Throughout his life, Paul travelled thousands of miles on foot and by ship. He entered cities, towns, and villages with nothing else than the message of God's love in Christ. He faced ridicule, violence, and prison but sought nothing in return except repentance and faith, resulting in disciples and churches wherever he went. Paul's churches were his hope and joy, the crown in which he will glory when the Lord Jesus comes (1 Thessalonians 2:19).

That's what motivated Paul to play his part in God's story.

YOUR PART IN GOD'S STORY

1. What are you learning about God and his mission?

_____

_____

_____

_____

_____

_____

2. How does God shape the people he calls?

_____

_____

_____

_____

_____

_____

_____

3. What is God saying to you about your part in his story?

_____

_____

_____

_____

_____

_____

_____

4. How will you think and act differently?

_____

_____

_____

_____

_____

_____

_____

*Because of
the increase of
wickedness, the
love of most will
grow cold, but the one
who stands firm to the
end will be saved. And this
gospel of the kingdom will be
preached in the whole world
as a testimony to all nations,
and then the end will come.*

MATTHEW 24:12—14

38

I FELL AT HIS FEET AS THOUGH DEAD

Read REVELATION 1—2:7

John was in exile on a small rocky island off the coast of what is now Turkey. Now an old man, probably in his eighties, he was caught up by the Spirit on the Lord's day when he heard a loud voice like a trumpet.

As he turned, he saw seven lampstands, and among them one like a son of man. Like Moses at the burning bush, Isaiah in the temple, and Paul on the Damascus road, the vision is overwhelming, and John fell to the ground as though dead. The One who has the keys of death and Hades reassured him, raised him to his feet, and commissioned him to write down what he saw and send it to the seven churches in the Roman province of Asia Minor. These seven churches represent all churches through the ages.[1]

There were seven lampstands in John's vision. At the center of Israel's worship in the holy place stood a candelabra bearing seven lamps.[2] Israel was meant to be the light of the world; now the churches of the new Israel are to be a light of witness to the world (Matthew 5:14).[3] The Risen Lord stands among the lampstands exalted in glory and power. The churches may be suffering persecution, but he is with them. He holds them in his hand, and each church is represented by an angelic being.

Christ is supreme. Jesus is the firstborn from the dead, the ruler of the kings of the earth, who loves his people and has freed them from their sins by his blood. He is the First and the Last, who is, and who was, and who is to come, the Almighty. He stands among the churches, as the glorious all-conquering Son of Man (Daniel 7:13–14).

Earlier, John reminded his readers of their identity: Jesus, the one who has freed them from their sins by his blood loves them, and he has made them to be a kingdom of priests to serve his God and Father (Exodus 19:6). As a kingdom of priests, they have direct access to God and are called to bring the light of his salvation to the world. As kings, they reign in the midst of suffering. They will conquer by refusing to compromise, by suffering as Christ did, and by defeating sin in their lives. They will defeat death and Satan by identifying with Jesus.[4] This is how they play their part in God's story.

Each letter to the churches begins by repeating some aspect of John's glorious vision of Christ (Revelation 2–3). Most of the letters add encouragement for the church's faithfulness under pressure. All the churches are besieged and threatened from within and without. The challenges and temptations they face are overwhelming and include: false apostles; a love for God that has grown cold; violent persecution; poverty; prison and the threat of execution; false teaching leading to idolatry and sexual immorality; toleration of false prophets; abandoning the gospel they first received; a lukewarm faith; and proud self-sufficiency.

Ephesus was founded by Paul around twenty-five to thirty years earlier. From Ephesus, the gospel went out, and churches were planted throughout the whole of Asia Minor (Acts 19:10). Before he left, Paul had warned the Ephesian elders that, after he departed, savage wolves would come among them that would endanger the flock (Acts 20:29).

Could any church have had a better foundation? Yet Paul's warning has been fulfilled: they have lost their first love and are in deadly peril.

The church at Ephesus is praised for its purity of belief but condemned for losing its first love and, with it, its desire to play its part in God's story. Jesus had warned his disciples that a time would come when most people's love would grow cold. They must endure to the end, for the gospel of the kingdom must be proclaimed to the whole world as a witness to the nations (Matthew 24:12–14). The Ephesians' love is failing, and they have no heart to reach a lost world. If the Ephesian church does not respond, it will be no more. Christ will remove their lampstand, and they will no longer be a witness to their world.[5]

The battle rages over and within the churches, a battle between Christ and the Antichrist for the hearts of humanity (Revelation 2–3). The threats to their existence are real: persecution and temptation from without; deception, immorality, and self-sufficiency from within. The churches have a vital part to play in this battle. They can become conquerors through loyalty to Christ, who has won the victory.

Christ both loves and disciplines these churches when they stray. If they do not respond, he will come to them in judgment. If they repent, he will transform them into the churches they are meant to be.

They have a part to play in God's story. Christ offers his people victory if they will listen to what the Spirit says to the churches. They will be given the right to eat from the tree of life, as well as hidden manna, a new name, authority over the nations, and having their names written in the book of life. They will be a pillar in the temple of God and have the right to sit with Christ on his throne![6]

Life will not make sense unless we understand we are in the midst of a cosmic battle. Eternity is at stake. God has a part for us to play in winning this war, but he will win it his way. He wages war, not relying on brute force and clever tactics. The final victory will be won by the Lamb who was slain.

YOUR PART IN GOD'S STORY

1. What are you learning about God and his mission?

_____

_____

_____

_____

_____

_____

_____

2. How does God shape the people he calls?

_____

_____

_____

_____

_____

_____

_____

3. What is God saying to you about your part in his story?

_____

_____

_____

_____

_____

_____

_____

4. How will you think and act differently?

_____

_____

_____

_____

_____

_____

_____

*Look, the Lamb
of God, who
takes away the sin
of the world!*

JOHN 1:29

39

THEN I SAW A LAMB

Read REVELATION 5

In a series of visions, the Apostle John was caught up into heaven. He saw a throne, and the One who sat upon it had the appearance of jasper and ruby. A rainbow that shone like an emerald surrounded the throne. From the throne came flashes of lightning, rumblings, and peals of thunder. Before "the throne, there was what looked like a sea of glass, clear as crystal" (Revelation 4:2–6).

Surrounding the throne were the elders, the living creatures, and a vast number of angels. Beyond them, the whole of creation was offering praise. They were waiting for One who will open the scroll that will unlock God's plan of redemption in history; the coming of the kingdom.

But no one can be found worthy to open the scroll and reveal its secrets. John weeps and weeps. Then the triumphant Lion of the tribe of Judah, the Root of David steps forward. He alone is able to open the scroll and its seven seals. John looks for this mighty Lion but instead sees a wounded Lamb.

Then heaven erupts into song as the worship of God gives way to the worship of the Lamb. The Lamb is worthy to take the scroll, open its seals, and reveal the heart of God's story. This is God's story from Genesis to Revelation. From beginning to end, this is the heart of God revealed in Jesus, his glory unveiled: a Lamb that was slain, whose blood purchased individuals for God from every tribe, language, and ethnicity. He has made them a kingdom of priests, who serve in his holy presence. Through the blood of a Lamb, God has triumphed over sin, death, and the devil. God's power has been revealed in the weakness of the cross.

This is the Lamb of God who takes away the sin of the world. This is the Suffering Servant, prophesied by Isaiah. This is the Passover lamb. The ram caught in the bushes who took the place of Isaac. This is the seed of the woman, who crushes the head of the Serpent. We're back in the garden; Eden is restored and surpassed, not by might but by a Lamb. The mission is completed, but the story does not end. A kingdom of priests will serve God and rule over a new heaven and new earth, united as one.

When Satan brought humanity crashing down, it could have ended there. If justice and might had prevailed, that would have ended humanity's rebellion. God was under no obligation to be merciful. His warning to Adam and Eve was clear: if they ate from the tree of the knowledge of good and evil, they would die. But God took the responsibility to put things right, even though he had done nothing wrong. God showed mercy and offered forgiveness and a new beginning. He's never stopped doing that. This is who he is. Just as he did with Adam, he comes looking and calling for each one of us, "Where are you?"

Mercy triumphs over justice, yet justice is upheld. God will take upon himself the sins of the world—the horror, the shame, the guilt. He will provide a Lamb to take our place. This is the key that unlocks God's story. We add nothing to the victory of the Lamb—how offensive that is to human pride! Yet God not only rescues us, he calls us to his cause. He gives us a part to play; his holy love shapes who we are and what we do.

All creation will worship him. His presence is our reward. Every tribe and tongue will worship him, and his love compels us to cry out to others, "Be reconciled to God!"

YOUR PART IN GOD'S STORY

1. What are you learning about God and his mission?

_____

_____

_____

_____

_____

_____

2. How does God shape the people he calls?

_____

_____

_____

_____

_____

_____

_____

3. What is God saying to you about your part in his story?

_____

_____

_____

_____

_____

_____

_____

4. How will you think and act differently?

_____

_____

_____

_____

_____

_____

_____

I heard a loud voice from the throne saying, "Look! God's dwelling place is now among the people, and he will dwell with them. They will be his people, and God himself will be with them and be their God."

REVELATION 21:3

40

I AM MAKING ALL THINGS NEW!

Read REVELATION 21

From beginning to end, the story of the Bible has a point. God has been on a mission to restore unbroken fellowship with men and women made in his image. God dwelt with Israel in the temple in Jerusalem. When the Word became flesh, God dwelt among us. God indwells his church, which is his temple, the body of Christ. All this anticipates the day when we will see him face to face.[1] Everything is summed up in this one statement: *God's dwelling place is now among the people.* God wants to be with us! This is the goal of redemption. This is when all the promises of God's covenants are fulfilled and surpassed.[2]

Genesis describes how God made the world. Revelation shows how he will remake it.[3] The heavenly Jerusalem will descend from heaven to take up its permanent location in the new earth.[4] Rebellious humanity tried to build a tower that would reach to the heavens, but this city comes down from God, not as a human achievement but as a gift. This new creation is a better Eden, a better Jerusalem, a better temple, in which God has established his glorious rule over all things and dwells in unbroken relationship with his people; a holy nation; a kingdom of priests.[5]

A sea of humanity from every tribe, tongue, and nation stands before the throne of God, giving glory to the Lamb that was slain. He will wipe away every tear; death will be no more. The city has no temple; the Lord God Almighty and the Lamb are its temple. The city gates are never shut, and all whose names are written in the Lamb's book of life may enter.

Finally, "the creation itself will be liberated from its bondage to decay and brought into the freedom and glory of the children of God" (Romans 8:21). Redeemed humanity is back in the garden, able to eat the bountiful fruit of the tree of life. The Serpent has been silenced. The curse has been removed, and God's people are again able to see his face and serve him.[6]

The whole city is God's dwelling place. This is not only a garden, but a garden-city, in which there is no temple. The gates are open to all the peoples of the world without distinction. "The only thing which disqualifies a man from entering the presence of God is sin; the only thing which will qualify him to enter is to have his name written in the book of life of the slain Lamb".[7] Without faith in Christ, people will spend eternity separated from God.

All mission will come to an end, and that end will be a total focus on the worship and the glory of God in our Lord Jesus Christ.[8] The time is near, yet the end is delayed.

God's glorious presence with his people in a transformed heaven and earth completes his plan of salvation. His presence is how he achieves his mission through us—God draws near to us and shapes us so that we can play our part in his story.[9] This is who God has made us to be; this is what he calls us to do.

The story ends with people from every tribe and nation enjoying his presence forever. In his grace, God includes us in his story.

There is still a job to do, and we have a part to play.

YOUR PART IN GOD'S STORY

1. What are you learning about God and his mission?

_____

_____

_____

_____

_____

_____

2. How does God shape the people he calls?

_____

_____

_____

_____

_____

_____

_____

3. What is God saying to you about your part in his story?

_____

_____

_____

_____

_____

_____

_____

_____

4. How will you think and act differently?

_____

_____

_____

_____

_____

_____

_____

_____

YOUR PART IN HOW THIS STORY ENDS

The Bible is full of stories that combine into the one story of God's plan to save a world that is in rebellion against him and stands under his judgment. God is the one who pursues us in the garden, calling out, "Where are you?" He promises that a descendant of the woman will come and forever silence the Serpent's lies. He chooses an old man and an old woman to be the unlikely parents of a nation that will be a light to the nations. When his people fail him, he promises a Servant King, a glorious Son of Man who will come and usher in the final age of salvation.

He declares God's kingship in a world in which evil reigns. The kingdoms of this world will pass away, but his kingdom will last forever. He doesn't come as a mighty ruler, who conquers with the sword, but as a Servant who suffers and dies alone at the hands of the people he came to save. The Savior dies, bearing the brunt and horror of our rebellion. God's wrath falls on him, and the damned go free. Victory is won by the Lamb that was slain.

He is the seed that fell to the ground and died, in order that it would produce life. His triumph is ours. Through him, heaven and earth will be made new. Seated at his Father's right hand, he poured out the Holy Spirit upon his people and sent them into the world to bring good news of salvation and the forgiveness of sin to all those who would end their rebellion and surrender to his love. They are his kingdom of priests, a holy nation, his bride, his precious possession, who are on a mission from Jerusalem to Judea, Samaria, and the ends of the earth. He eagerly awaits the day when he will return in glory to complete his mission.

We know how the story ends: a new heaven and a new earth; Eden restored and surpassed; a holy city, the new Jerusalem, coming down out of heaven from God.

Jesus stands ready. Yet he waits. This gospel of repentance for the forgiveness of sins—this gospel of the kingdom—will be preached throughout the whole world in his name, and then the end will come.

We know how the story ends.

The question is, what part will you play?

LESSONS FROM THE 40-DAY CHALLENGE

1. What have you learnt about God and his mission?

_____

_____

_____

_____

_____

_____

2. How does God shape the people he calls?

_____

_____

_____

_____

_____

_____

_____

3. How is God shaping you?

_____

_____

_____

_____

_____

_____

_____

4. What is God saying to you about your part in his story?

_____

_____

_____

_____

_____

_____

_____

5. How will you think and act differently?

_____

_____

_____

_____

_____

_____

_____

6. Who will you partner with?

_____

_____

_____

_____

_____

_____

_____

7. What will you do next?

_____

_____

_____

_____

_____

_____

_____

_____

TAKE THE 40-DAY CHALLENGE

Individual Challenge

Set aside at least thirty minutes a day for forty days to discover your part in God's story. Each day:

1. Read the passage.
2. Read the reflection.
3. Write out your answers to the four discovery questions:

   - What are you learning about God and his mission?
   - How does God shape the people he calls?
   - What is God saying to you about your part in his story?
   - How will you think and act differently?

At the end of the forty days:

Complete the final exercise: Lessons from the 40-Day Challenge.

Group Challenge

Each group member commits to the Individual Challenge above. Meet weekly in groups of two to five people. If you have more than five people, break into subgroups that report back.

Meet for ninety minutes to:

1. Review your progress.
2. Share what you are learning.
3. Talk about how you are thinking and acting differently.
4. Complete that day's study as a group.

At the end of the forty days:

Meet to discuss the final exercise: Lessons from the 40-Day Challenge.

Plan how, individually and as a group, you will play your part in God's story.

Journey Together

Get updates and stay in touch with others on the 40-Day Challenge by registering your commitment at:

movements.net/40days

NOTES

With Jesus on the Road to Emmaus

1   Andreas J. Köstenberger and Peter T. O'Brien, *Salvation to the Ends of the Earth: A Biblical Theology of Mission*, vol. 11, ed. D. A. Carson, New Studies in Biblical Theology (Downers Grove, IL: InterVarsity Press, 2001), 52.

2   Luke 9:16, 22:19.

3   Luke 23:49.

4   Mark 9:33–36; Luke 9:46–47.

5   Robert C. Tannehill, *The Gospel According to Luke*, vol. 1, The Narrative Unity of Luke–Acts: A Literary Interpretation (Philadelphia: Fortress Press, 1991), 274.

6   Ian M. Duguid, *Ezekiel*, The NIV Application Commentary (Grand Rapids: Zondervan Academic, 1999), 38.

7   Luke 24:45–48.

8   You'll find a list of the other books I've written on movements at the end of this book.

1: The Beginning

1   Stephen G. Dempster, *Dominion and Dynasty: A Theology of the Hebrew Bible*, vol. 15, ed. D. A. Carson, New Studies in Biblical Theology (Downers Grove, IL: InterVarsity Press, 2003), 56.

2   Waltke and Yu comment, "The garden, by extension, is a temple—God is uniquely present in a way he is not elsewhere. In this garden people meet God and walk and talk with him. As a temple, it is the axis between heaven and earth. Its sanctity is protected by cherubim (Gen. 3:24; Exod. 26:1; 2 Chron. 3:7) so that sin and death

are excluded." Bruce K. Waltke with Charles Yu, *An Old Testament Theology: An Exegetical, Canonical, and Thematic Approach* (Grand Rapids: Zondervan, 2007), 255.

3   Dempster writes, "It is as if humanity is functioning as a type of priest-king, mediating God to the world and the world to God." Dempster, *Dominion and Dynasty*, 62.

4   Thomas R. Schreiner, *The King in His Beauty: A Biblical Theology of the Old and New Testaments* (Grand Rapids: Baker Academic, 2013), 6–7.

5   Dempster, *Dominion and Dynasty*, 59.

6   Richard Bauckham, *Bible and Mission: Christian Witness in a Postmodern World* (Carlisle, UK: Paternoster, 2003), 35.

7   Andreas J. Köstenberger with T. Desmond Alexander, *Salvation to the Ends of the Earth: A Biblical Theology of Mission*, vol. 53, 2nd ed., ed. D. A. Carson, New Studies in Biblical Theology (Downers Grove, IL: InterVarsity Press, 2020), 13.

8   T. Desmond Alexander, *From Eden to the New Jerusalem: An Introduction to Biblical Theology* (Grand Rapids: Kregel Academic, 2008), 27.

9   Köstenberger and Alexander, *Salvation to the Ends of the Earth*, 14.

2: We'll Make a Name for Ourselves

1   See Genesis 4:1–16.

2   Dempster, *Dominion and Dynasty*, 72.

3   Alexander, *From Eden to the New Jerusalem*, 29.

4   Bruce K. Waltke with Cathi J. Fredricks, *Genesis: A Commentary* (Grand Rapids: Zondervan Academic, 2001), 178.

5   Gordon John Wenham, *Genesis 1–15*, vol. 1, ed. David A. Hubbard, Glenn Barker, and John D. W. Watts, Word Biblical Commentary (Waco, TX: Word Books, 1987), 335.

6   Daniel 3; Isaiah 47:8–13; Revelation 17–18.

7   Christopher J. H. Wright, *The Mission of God: Unlocking the Bible's Grand Narrative* (Downers Grove, IL: IVP Academic, 2006), 199.

3: Father of a Nation

[1] Originally Abraham was called Abram. His name was changed when God reaffirmed his promises (Genesis 15:5). His wife Sarah was originally Sarai.

[2] See Walter C. Kaiser Jr., *Mission in the Old Testament: Israel as a Light to the Nations*, 2nd ed. (Grand Rapids, MI: Baker Academic, 2012), 10.

[3] Deuteronomy 26:5; Joshua 24:2.

[4] Schreiner, *The King in His Beauty*, 19–20.

[5] Derek Kidner, *Genesis: An Introduction and Commentary*, ed. D. J. Wiseman, Tyndale Old Testament Commentaries (Leicester, UK: Inter-Varsity Press, 1967), 113.

[6] Gordon John Wenham, *Genesis 16–50*, vol. 2, ed. David A. Hubbard, Glenn Barker, and John D. W. Watts, Word Biblical Commentary (Grand Rapids: Zondervan Academic, 2000), 117.

[7] Romans 4.

4: Out of Egypt

[1] W. Ross Blackburn, *The God Who Makes Himself Known: The Missionary Heart of the Book of Exodus*, ed. D. A. Carson, New Studies in Biblical Theology (Downers Grove, IL: InterVarsity Press, 2012), 49.

[2] Alexander, *From Eden to the New Jerusalem*, 128.

[3] Blackburn, *The God Who Makes Himself Known*, 50.

5: A Kingdom of Priests

[1] Köstenberger and Alexander, *Salvation to the Ends of the Earth,* 34.

[2] Blackburn, *The God Who Makes Himself Known*, 93.

[3] In Matthew 22:36–40 Jesus is quoting Deuteronomy 6:5 and Leviticus 19:18.

4   Schreiner, *The King in His Beauty*, 38.

5   Bauckham, *Bible and Mission*, 36.

6   Leviticus 26, Deuteronomy 27–28.

7   Blackburn, *The God Who Makes Himself Known*, 103.

8   Blackburn, *The God Who Makes Himself Known*, 103. Hedlund comments, "The nations are tribes, ethnic groups, peoples surrounding Israel, each with a distinctive culture and identity. Theologically, they are the peoples without the knowledge of the true and living God." Roger E. Hedlund, *The Mission of the Church in the World: A Biblical Theology* (Grand Rapids, MI: Baker Books, 1985), 67.

6: Your Throne Will Last Forever

1   Dempster, *Dominion and Dynasty*, 142.

2   Schreiner, *The King in His Beauty*, 157.

7: You Are My Son

1   VanGemeren comments, "God's relationship with David and his sons, who were also 'anointed,' involves the promise that through the Davidic dynasty God will establish his universal rule over the earth." Willem A. VanGemeren, *Psalms*, rev. ed., The Expositor's Bible Commentary (Grand Rapids: Zondervan Academic), 89.

2   Peter C. Craigie, *Psalms 1–50*, vol. 19, ed. Temper Longman III and David E. Garland, Word Biblical Commentary (Waco, TX: Word, 1983), 65.

3   In this section I'm following Bauckham, *Bible and Mission*, 46.

4   Bauckham, *Bible and Mission*, 48.

5   Craigie, *Psalms 1–50*, 67.

8: I Saw the Lord

1   1 Kings 12. After the death of King Solomon (around 930 BC) the nation split into a northern kingdom, which kept the name Israel, and

a southern kingdom called Judah, named after the tribe of Judah. See F. F. Bruce, *Israel and the Nations: From the Exodus to the Fall of the Second Temple* (Exeter, UK: Paternoster, 1963), 39–40.

[2]   2 Chronicles 26. See John N. Oswalt, *The Book of Isaiah: Chapters 1–39*, The New International Commentary on the Old Testament (Grand Rapids: Eerdmans, 1986), 177.

[3]   "'Sitting upon a throne' does more than indicate a king who is in power. The throne is the place for executing judgment. As Brettler puts it, 'God's throne is specifically associated with his role as judge.'" Andrew T. Abernethy, *The Book of Isaiah and God's Kingdom: A Thematic-Theological Approach*, vol. 40, ed. D. A. Carson, New Studies in Biblical Theology (Downers Grove, IL: IVP Academic, 2016), Kindle edition, Kindle location 554.

[4]   Jeremiah 34:16; Amos 2:7.

[5]   Oswalt, *Isaiah 1–39*, 181.

[6]   Abernethy, *The Book of Isaiah and God's Kingdom*, Kindle location 554.

[7]   Oswalt, *Isaiah 1–39*, 183.

[8]   Oswalt, *Isaiah 1–39*, 184.

[9]   Leviticus 18:25–27; Deuteronomy 28. Oswalt, *Isaiah 1–39*, 190.

[10]   Dempster, *Dominion and Dynasty*, 181.

9: Here Is My Servant

[1]   The curse of exile was prophesied by Moses in Leviticus 26 and Deuteronomy 28–32 and by Solomon in 1 Kings 8. The prophets repeated Moses' warnings in Isaiah 39:6–7; Hosea 11:5; Amos 5:27.

[2]   Barry Webb, *The Message of Isaiah: On Eagles' Wings*, ed. Alec Motyer, The Bible Speaks Today (Nottingham, UK: Inter-Varsity Press, 1996), 170.

[3]   Webb, *Isaiah*, 212–13.

[4]   According to Leviticus, the animal sacrificed as a sin offering "bears" or "takes away" the guilt of the community (Leviticus 10:17). On

the annual Day of Atonement, the guilt of the community is placed on the scapegoat, which is chased out into the desert bearing it away (Leviticus 16:22). See Paul R. House, *Old Testament Theology* (Downers Grove, IL: InterVarsity Press, 1998), 291.

5   Dempster, *Dominion and Dynasty*, 178.

6   Webb, *Isaiah*, 213.

7   Isaiah 54:17; 56:6; 63:17; 65:8–15; 66:14. See Abernethy, *The Book of Isaiah*, Kindle Location 2946.

10: The Valley of Dry Bones

1   Leviticus 18:25–27; Deuteronomy 28.

2   L. S. Tiemeyer, "Ezekiel: Book Of," in *Dictionary of The Old Testament Prophets*, ed. Mark J. Boda and J. Gordon McConville (Downers Grove, IL: IVP Academic, 2012), 221.

3   Daniel I. Block, *The Book of Ezekiel: Chapters 25–48*, The New International Commentary on the Old Testament (Grand Rapids: Eerdmans, 1998), 374.

4   Ezekiel 36:26–27; Jeremiah 31:31–34.

11: One Like a Son of Man

1   The final destruction of Jerusalem did not occur until 597 BC following a failed rebellion. See Bruce, *Israel and the Nations*, 86–92.

2   Joyce Baldwyn writes, "The first year of Belshazzar would be 552/551 BC, over fifty years since Daniel's deportation to Babylon." Joyce G. Baldwyn, *Daniel: An Introduction and Commentary*, Tyndale Old Testament Commentaries (Leicester, UK: Inter-Varsity Press, 1978), 138.

3   Dempster, *Dominion and Dynasty*, 215.

4   Dempster, *Dominion and Dynasty*, 217.

5   Authority to forgive sins: Matthew 9:6; Lord of the Sabbath: Matthew 12:8; predicted suffering and death: Mark 10:31–34; predicted vindication and return: Luke 22:69.

12: Should I Not Care for This Great City?

1. James Bruckner, *Jonah, Nahum, Habakkuk, Zephaniah*, The NIV Application Commentary (Grand Rapids: Zondervan Academic, 2004), 28–29.
2. Leslie C. Allen, *The Books of Joel, Obadiah, Jonah and Micah*, The New International Commentary on the Old Testament (Grand Rapids: Eerdmans, 1976), 178.
3. Johannes Verkuyl, "The Biblical Foundation for the Worldwide Mission Mandate," in *Perspectives on the World Christian Movement*, 3rd ed., Ralph D. Winter and Steven C. Hawthorne (Pasadena, CA: William Carey Library, 1999), 32.
4. Bruckner, *Jonah*, 128.
5. Bruckner, *Jonah*, 130–131.

13: In the Beginning Was the Word

1. Leon Morris, *The Gospel According to John*, ed. F. F. Bruce, New International Commentary on the New Testament (Grand Rapids: Eerdmans, 1971), 74.
2. Gary M. Burge, *John*, vol. 4, The NIV Application Commentary (Grand Rapids: Zondervan Academic, 2000), Kindle edition, Kindle location 944.
3. Michael Reeves, *Delighting in the Trinity: An Introduction to the Christian Faith* (Downers Grove, IL: IVP Academic, 2012), 24–26.
4. Genesis 1:3. See Reeves, *Delighting in the Trinity*, 50.
5. John 12:23–24; 13:31.
6. John 3:3. Morris, *The Gospel According to John*, 98.
7. Exodus 33:18–20. Herman N. Ridderbos, *The Gospel of John: A Theological Commentary*, trans. John Vriend (Grand Rapids: Eerdmans, 1997), 57.
8. Lister, writes, "The first truth is this: the presence of God is a central goal in God's redemptive mission. The second truth follows: the presence of God is the agent by which the Lord accomplishes his

redemptive mission." J. Ryan Lister, *The Presence of God: Its Place in the Storyline of Scripture and the Story of Our Lives* (Wheaton, IL: Crossway, 2015), 23–24.

9   Burge, *John*, Kindle location 1239.

14: The Day It Began

1   Isaiah 40–55.

2   Luke 3:22 combines Psalm 2:7 and Isaiah 42:1.

15: The Spirit of the Lord Is Upon Me

1   Leon Morris, *The Cross in the New Testament* (Exeter, UK: Paternoster, 1965), 56.

2   Peter T. O'Brien, "Mission, Witness, and the Coming of the Spirit," *Bulletin for Biblical Research* 9 (1999), 203.

3   In the Old Testament the poor include true Israel oppressed by conquest and foreign domination at the hand of God. See O'Brien, "Mission," 206, and David Peter Seccombe, *Possessions and the Poor in Luke–Acts* (Linz, Austria: SNTU, 1982).

4   Luke 13:16; Acts 10:38.

5   Joel B. Green, *The Gospel of Luke*, ed. Gordon D. Fee, New International Commentary on the New Testament (Grand Rapids: Eerdmans, 1997), 211.

6   Green, *The Gospel of Luke*, 212.

7   1 Kings 17:8–24; 2 Kings 5:1–19.

16: Fishing for People

1   A boat that was discovered buried in the silt of the lake after a prolonged dry season in modern-day Israel when the sea level had receded, and carbon-dated from 120 BC to AD 40, may be similar to the boats these fishermen used. It measured 25.5 feet long, 7.5 feet wide, and 4.5 feet in depth. It had a deck in the bow and the stern and could

be powered by sails or by four oars. It normally had a crew of five with a capacity for ten passengers or an excess of a ton of cargo. Three types of nets were used: the seine net (Matthew 13:47–48), the cast net (Mark 1:16), and the trammel net, which could stretch to 500 feet and required two boats working together to pull it. See David E. Garland, *Luke*, ed. Clinton E. Arnold, Zondervan Exegetical Commentary on the New Testament, Kindle edition, Kindle locations 5261–5267.

[2] Matthew 12:46–50; Mark 3:31–35; 10:29–30.

17: Four Soils

[1] Eckhard J. Schnabel, *Mark: An Introduction and Commentary*, vol. 2, Tyndale New Testament Commentaries (Downers Grove, IL: IVP Academic, 2017), 9.

[2] C. E. B. Cranfield, *The Gospel According to St Mark: An Introduction and Commentary*, ed. C. F. D. Moule, The Cambridge Greek Testament Commentary (London: Cambridge University Press, 1959), 151.

[3] Cranfield, *The Gospel According to St Mark*, 153.

[4] Mark 4:12; Isaiah 6:9–10.

[5] Mark 5; Luke 7:1-10.

[6] James R. Edwards, *The Gospel According to Mark*, ed. D. A. Carson, The Pillar New Testament Commentary (Grand Rapids, MI: Eerdmans, 2002), 138.

[7] David E. Garland, *Luke*, Kindle locations 8104–8105.

[8] Edwards, *The Gospel According to Mark*, 133.

[9] David E. Garland, *A Theology of Mark's Gospel: Good News about Jesus the Messiah, the Son of God*, ed. Andreas J. Köstenberger, Biblical Theology of the New Testament (Grand Rapids: Zondervan, 2015), Kindle edition, Kindle location 11006.

[10] Luke 18:18–30.

[11] William L. Lane, *The Gospel of Mark: An Exegetical and Theological Exposition of Holy Scripture*, vol. 23, ed. F. F. Bruce, New International Commentary on the New Testament (Grand Rapids: Eerdmans, 1974), 158.

[12] James A. Brooks, *Mark*, ed. David S. Dockery, The New American Commentary 23 (Nashville: Broadman & Holman, 1991), Kindle edition, Kindle locations 1929–1932.

18: On the Road

[1] D. A. Carson, "Matthew," in *Matthew, Mark, Luke*, vol. 8, ed. Frank E. Gaebelein, Expositor's Bible Commentary with the New International Version of the Holy Bible (Grand Rapids: Zondervan, 1984), 244.
[2] Carson, "Matthew," 246.
[3] Matthew 8:11–12; 11:20–24.
[4] Examples: 2 Corinthians 11:24; Acts 7:55; 25.

19: Sheep and Goats

[1] Daniel 7:13–14; Zechariah 14:5.
[2] Carson, "Matthew," 521.
[3] Carson, "Matthew," 521.
[4] R. T. France, *The Gospel of Matthew*, ed. Gordon D. Fee, New International Commentary on the New Testament (Grand Rapids: Eerdmans, 2007), 961–962.
[5] Carson, "Matthew," 520.

20: Remain in Me

[1] Colin G. Kruse, *The Gospel of John: An Introduction and Commentary*, Tyndale New Testament Commentaries (Leicester, UK: Inter-Varsity Press, 2003), 314.
[2] See also Psalm 80:9–16; Isaiah 27:2; Jeremiah 2:21; 12:10; Ezekiel 15:1–8; 17:1–21; 19:10–14; Hosea 10:1–2.
[3] Burge, *John*, Kindle location 8548.
[4] Kruse, *The Gospel of John*, 319.
[5] Kruse, *The Gospel of John*, 322, and Morris, *The Gospel According to John*, 676.

6   2 Chronicles 20:7; Isaiah 41:8; Exodus 33:11.

21: Expect Trouble

1   See John 16:1.
2   I'm following Chee-Chiew Lee, "A Theology of Facing Persecution in the Gospel of John," *Tyndale Bulletin* 2, no. 70 (2019), 185–204.

22: Drenched

1   See John 7.
2   For the background on the Feast see D. A. Carson, *The Gospel According to John*, The Pillar New Testament Commentary (Grand Rapids, MI: Eerdmans, 1991), Kindle edition, Kindle location 6582. Also, Morris, *The Gospel According to John*, 420.
3   Kruse, *The Gospel of John*, 304.

23: Surrender

1   Luke 22:39; John 18:2.
2   Lane, *The Gospel of Mark*, 515.
3   Eckhard J. Schnabel, *Jesus in Jerusalem: The Last Days* (Grand Rapids: Eerdmans, 2018), 224.
4   Numbers 4:14; Exodus 24:6.
5   Carl J. Armbruster, "The Messianic Significance of the Agony in the Garden," *Scripture*, no. 16 (1964), 114.
6   Lane, *The Gospel of Mark*, 517.
7   Schnabel, *Jesus in Jerusalem*, 225.
8   See Garland, *A Theology of Mark's Gospel*, Kindle location 10465.

24: My God, My God!

1   Peter G. Bolt, *The Cross from a Distance: Atonement in Mark's Gospel*, vol. 18, ed. D. A. Carson, New Studies in Biblical Theology

(Downers Grove, IL: InterVarsity Press, 2004), 54. See Ezekiel 39:23.

2   Exodus 10:21–22; Deuteronomy 28:29.

3   Bolt, *The Cross from a Distance*, 135.

4   Deuteronomy 21:22–23.

5   Bolt, *The Cross from a Distance*, 140–41.

6   Bolt, *The Cross from a Distance*, 141.

25: He Opened Their Minds

1   See Green, *The Gospel of Luke*, 844.

2   Tannehill, *The Gospel According to Luke*, 294.

3   Luke 3:3; Mark 1:15.

4   Tannehill, *The Gospel According to Luke*, 297. Later Paul summarised his mission as proclaiming repentance to God and faith in our Lord Jesus (Acts 20:21).

5   Alan J. Thompson, *The Acts of the Risen Lord Jesus: Luke's Account of God's Unfolding Plan*, vol. 27, New Studies in Biblical Theology (Downers Grove, IL: IVP, 2011), 17.

6   See Genesis 3:15; Isaiah 2:3; Micah 4:2; Genesis 12:1–3; Isaiah 49:6.

26: Make Disciples of All Nations

1   Hedlund, *The Mission of the Church in the World*, 67.

2   Carson, "Matthew," 597.

3   Leon Morris, *The Gospel According to Matthew*, The Pillar New Testament Commentary (Grand Rapids, MI: Eerdmans, 1992), 750.

4   Köstenberger and Alexander, *Salvation to the Ends of the Earth*, 67.

27: You Will Receive Power

1   For the dating of Pentecost see, Eckhard J. Schnabel, *Early Christian Mission: Jesus and the Twelve*, vol. 1 (Downers Grove, IL: IVP Academic, 2004), 389.

2   Michael Green, *Evangelism in the Early Church* (London: Hodder & Stoughton, 1970), 149.

3   Lister, *The Presence of God*, 304.

28: The First Church

1   David G. Peterson, *The Acts of the Apostles*, Pillar New Testament Commentary (Grand Rapids: Eerdmans, 2009), 154.

2   The term "kingdom" occurs forty-two times in Luke's Gospel but just eight times in his book of Acts. Importantly the term "kingdom" appears at the very beginning of Acts and at the end (Acts 1:3, 28:31) and also appears throughout Acts. Chris Green maintains that Acts is a commentary on the kingdom of God. Right now, the reality of the kingdom can be experienced through repentance and faith. The gospel of the kingdom is not an alternative to the gospel of Christ crucified for our sin. Jesus has been sent not only to announce the coming reign of God, but to perform the decisive event through which God will bring in that reign. Talking about the kingdom of God requires us to talk about the cross. See Chris Green, "The King, His Kingdom and the Gospel: Matthew, Mark and Luke–Acts" in *God's Power to Save: One Gospel for a Complex World?*, ed. Chris Green (Leicester, UK: Inter-Varsity Press, 2006), 104–37.

3   See Robert H. Stein, "Baptism and Becoming a Christian in the New Testament," *Southern Baptist Journal of Theology*, 2/1 (1998), 6–17.

4   Eckhard J. Schnabel, *Acts*, ed. Clinton E. Arnold, Zondervan Exegetical Commentary on the New Testament (Grand Rapids: Zondervan, 2012), 179.

5   According to Schnabel, we know of forty-six people by name who belonged to the community of believers in Jerusalem at any time before AD 70. In addition to the Twelve (Acts 1:13, 26), the Seven (Acts 6:5), and the brothers of Jesus as well as Mary, Jesus' mother (Acts 1:14), the list includes names such as Agabus, the prophet; John Mark, eventually a missionary who traveled with Barnabas and Paul; Joseph Barnabas, later a missionary in Syria and in Cyprus;

Joseph of Arimathea, an aristocrat and member of the Sanhedrin; Nicodemus, another aristocrat and member of the Sanhedrin; Silas–Silvanus, later a missionary coworker of Paul; Simon of Cyrene, who had helped to carry Jesus' cross; and Addai, the first missionary in Edessa. See Schnabel, *Acts*, 185.

29: Persecution and Power

[1] John Stott, *The Message of Acts: To the Ends of the Earth*, 2nd ed., The Bible Speaks Today (Leicester, UK: Inter-Varsity Press, 1991), 100.
[2] Acts 4:31; 8:4; 11:19.

30: Eating Dust on the Damascus Road

[1] Schnabel, *Early Christian Mission*, 51.
[2] Peterson, *The Acts of the Apostles*, 302.
[3] Schnabel, *Acts*, 445.
[4] Schnabel, *Acts*, 445.
[5] Acts 9; 22; 26.
[6] Adapted from Robert C. Tannehill, *The Acts of the Apostles*, vol. 2, The Narrative Unity of Luke–Acts: A Literary Interpretation (Minneapolis: Fortress Press, 1990), 119–20.
[7] Peterson, *The Acts of the Apostles*, 309.

31: The Work

[1] Eckhard J. Schnabel, *Paul the Missionary: Realities, Strategies and Methods* (Downers Grove, IL: IVP Academic, 2008), 74–75.
[2] Schnabel, *Paul the Missionary*, 264.
[3] Schnabel, *Acts*, 619.
[4] According to Polhill they could have continued southeast from Derbe, on through the Cilician gates, and traveled the one hundred and fifty miles or so to Paul's hometown of Tarsus and from there back to Syrian Antioch. It would have been the easiest route home by

far. John B. Polhill, *Acts: An Exegetical and Theological Exposition of Holy Scripture*, vol. 26, The New American Commentary (Nashville, TN: Broadman & Holman, 1992), 318.

5   Acts 13:5–7, 44–49; 14:25.

6   Acts 13:13–43; 14:15–17.

7   Schnabel, *Acts*, 561.

32: To Live Is Christ, to Die Is Gain

1   According to Schnabel, "Paul's missionary work in Philippi (Acts 16:12–40) probably took place in the months of August and October of AD 49." Schnabel, *Paul the Missionary*, 92.

2   Acts 28:16. Paul would have been lightly chained and living somewhere near the Praetorian barracks. See Brian Rapske, *Paul in Roman Custody*, vol. 3, The Book of Acts in Its First Century Setting (Grand Rapids: Eerdmans, 2004), 173–191.

3   Rome is the traditional location for the writing of this letter. Other cities such as Ephesus and Caesarea are also proposed. See Gerald F. Hawthorne, *Philippians*, vol. 43, Word Biblical Commentary (Waco, TX: Word Books, 1983), xxxvi–xliv.

4   For Paul's partnership with the Philippians see Philippians 1:5,19; 4:14–20.

5   Philippians 1:13; 4:22. The soldiers of the Praetorian Guard—the emperor's personal bodyguards—had sixteen cohorts of a thousand men. Their role was to protect the emperor and his family, and to discourage and suppress plots and disturbances. They were at the very heart of the Roman Empire. Over the two years, many of these legionnaires would have heard the gospel from Paul, and some passed it on to their comrades.

Paul mentions there were believers in "the emperor's household" (Philippians 4:22). The household of a Roman aristocrat included his family, servants, slaves, and freedmen. Often their duties were specialized, such as domestic servants and professionals providing medical, commercial, and secretarial help. Caesar's household was equivalent to a modern civil service based in Rome but also in households scattered throughout the provinces. Members of Caesar's household were powerful and socially mobile, despite being slaves and former slaves. See Steve Addison, *What Jesus Started: Joining the Movement, Changing the World* (Downers Grove, IL: InterVarsity Press, 2012), 130–1, 158–159.

6 James P. Ware, *Paul and the Mission of the Church: Philippians in Ancient Jewish Context* (Grand Rapids: Baker Academic, 2011), Kindle edition, Kindle locations 2222–2225.

7 Ware, *Paul and the Mission*, Kindle locations 3022–3030.

33: What Is Apollos? And What Is Paul?

1 I have relied on Schnabel, *Paul the Missionary*, 130–135, for what follows.

2 Acts 18 tells the story of Paul's mission to Corinth. Later Paul wrote to the believers in Corinth and to all God's people throughout the surrounding region of Achaia (2 Corinthians 1:1).

3 Mark 10:41–45; Luke 22:25–27.

4 Gordon D. Fee, *The First Epistle to the Corinthians*, vol. 7, ed. F. F. Bruce, The New International Commentary on the New Testament (Grand Rapids: Eerdmans, 1987), 132.

5 Craig L. Blomberg, *1 Corinthians*, The NIV Application Commentary (Zondervan, 1994), 39–40.

6 Gold, silver, and precious stones describe the building materials of Solomon's temple (1 Chronicles 29:2).

7 Fee, *The First Epistle to the Corinthians*, 146.

8 Fee, *The First Epistle to the Corinthians*, 149.

34: The Power of Weakness

1 He uses the same word when he refers to the Serpent who questioned God's Word and deceived Eve by his "cunning" (2 Corinthians 11:3).

2 Acts 9:1–19; Galatians 1:13–17.

3   2 Corinthians 1:14; Philippians 2:16; 1 Thessalonians 2:19.

4   Paul Barnett, *The Second Epistle to the Corinthians*, ed. Gordon D. Fee, The New International Commentary on the New Testament (Grand Rapids, MI: Eerdmans, 1997), 252.

35: The Fight

1   Schnabel, *Paul the Missionary*, 110.

2   Peter T. O'Brien, *The Letter to the Ephesians*, ed. D. A. Carson, The Pillar New Testament Commentary (Grand Rapids: Eerdmans, 1999), 56.

3   Clinton E. Arnold, *Ephesians*, Zondervan Exegetical Commentary on the New Testament (Grand Rapids: Zondervan, 2010), Kindle edition, Kindle location 12970.

4   Arnold, *Ephesians*, Kindle location 12441.

5   See Ephesians 2:1–10.

6   O'Brien, *The Letter to the Ephesians*, 482.

7   Clinton E. Arnold, *Powers of Darkness: Principalities & Powers in Paul's Letters* (Downers Grove, IL: InterVarsity Press, 1992), Kindle edition, Kindle location 1876.

8   O'Brien, *The Letter to the Ephesians*, 483–484.

9   Romans 8:26–27.

36: Looking Back

1   Schnabel, *Acts*, 45.

2   See Acts 19:10. The churches were planted by his coworker Epaphras (Colossians 1:3–8; 2:1; 4:13). See Addison, *What Jesus Started*, 154–158.

3   Peterson, *Acts*, 565.

4   Peterson, *Acts*, 568.

5   Acts 20:4 lists Sopater, son of Pyrrhus from Berea; Aristarchus and Secundus from Thessalonica; Gaius from Derbe; Timothy, Tychicus and Trophimus from the province of Asia.

37: I Am Not Ashamed

1   Leon Morris, *The Epistle to the Romans,* The Pillar New Testament Commentary (Grand Rapids, MI: Eerdmans, 1988), 76.

2   Moo writes, "Those who ignore or minimize the problem inherent in a holy God accepting sinners may well heed Anselm's own warning: 'You have not yet considered the weight of sin.'" Douglas J. Moo, *The Epistle to the Romans*, ed. Gordon D. Fee, New International Commentary on the New Testament (Grand Rapids, MI: Eerdmans, 1996), 242.

3   Moo, *The Epistle to the Romans*, 106–7.

4   Moo, *The Epistle to the Romans*, 98.

5   Moo, *The Epistle to the Romans*, 74.

38: I Fell at His Feet as Though Dead

1   George Eldon Ladd, *A Commentary on the Revelation of John* (Grand Rapids, MI: Eerdmans, 1972), 24.

2   Exodus 25:37; Zechariah 4:2.

3   G. K. Beale with David H. Campbell, *Revelation: A Shorter Commentary* (Grand Rapids: Eerdmans, 2015), 55.

4   Beale and Campbell, *Revelation*, 46.

5   The church is the lampstand (Revelation 1:20), and God and the Lamb are the lamps (Revelation 21:23–24; 22:5). See Beale, *Revelation*, 56.

6   Revelation 2–3 contains the following: eat from the tree of life, 2:7; manna and new name, 2:17; authority over nations, 2:26; names in the book of life, 3:5; a pillar in God's temple, 3:12; with Christ on his throne, 3:21.

40: I Am Making All Things New!

1   Revelation 22:4.

2   Ladd, *A Commentary on the Revelation of John*, 277.

3   Michael Wilcock, *I Saw Heaven Opened: The Message of Revelation,*

ed. John Stott, The Bible Speaks Today (Leicester, UK: Inter-Varsity Press, 1975), 212.

4   Ladd, *A Commentary on the Revelation of John*, 275.

5   Lister, *The Presence of God*, 6.

6   Rev 22:1–4. Robert H. Mounce, *The Book of Revelation*, ed. Gordon D. Fee, rev. ed., The New International Commentary on the New Testament (Grand Rapids: Eerdmans, 1998), Kindle edition, Kindle location 7234.

7   Wilcock, *I Saw Heaven Opened*, 210.

8   O'Brien and Köstenberger, *Salvation to the Ends of the Earth*, 262.

9   I'm indebted to Lister for these reflections on the presence of God as the goal and the means of God's redemptive mission. Lister, *The Presence of God*, 22.

STEVE ADDISON is a catalyst for movements that multiply disciples and churches everywhere. He is a missions leader, author, speaker, and mentor to pioneers.

Steve is married to Michelle. They live in Melbourne, Australia and have four children and two and a half grandchildren. Michelle and Steve lead MOVE, a mission agency devoted to training and deploying workers who multiply disciples and churches.

Also by Steve Addison

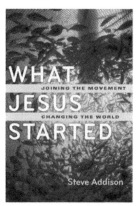

With a sensitivity to history and an ability to extract principles from the lives of the apostolic pioneers who have gone before us, Steve gives us an inspirational peek into movements and the people who lead them.

ALAN HIRSCH

Stay in Touch

Access articles, video and podcast interviews, and
training resources here:

movements.net

Lightning Source UK Ltd.
Milton Keynes UK
UKHW011824300321
381271UK00001B/91

9 781735 598895